GROUNDED
IN THE WORD

GROUNDED IN THE WORD:

A GUIDE TO

MASTERING STANDARDIZED

TEST VOCABULARY AND

BIBLICAL COMPREHENSION

Comptex Associates, Incorporated
P.O. Box 6745
Washington, D.C. 20020

Copyright ©1997 by Eugene Williams, Sr. and Eugene Williams, Jr.
Comptex Associates, Incorporated
P.O. Box 6745, Washington, D.C. 20020
All rights reserved.
No part of this book may be reproduced or transmitted
in any form or by any means, electronic or mechanical,
including photocopying, recording, or by any information
storage and retrieval system without permission in writing
from the publisher.

ISBN: 0-911849-06-8

Printed in the United States of America
Second Edition

Request for information about the author's availability for
speaking engagements and workshops for high school and
college students should be addressed to:

>   Comptex Associates, Inc.
>   P.O. Box 6745
>   Washington, D.C. 20020
>   (301) 599-9222
>   E-Mail: comptex@webtv.net

WORD LIST

WORD	CHAPTER	VERSE	BOOK	PAGE
ABASED	4	12	PHILIPPIANS	289
ABASHED	3	7	MICAH	223
ABHORRENT	5	21	EXODUS	46
ABOMINATION	43	32	GENESIS	39
ABOUND	1	9	PHILIPPIANS	289
ADAMANT	3	9	EZEKIEL	191
ADJOIN	49	13	GENESIS	41
ADJOURNED	24	22	ACTS	262
ADMONISHED	12	12	ECCLESIASTES	159
ADORNED	9	30	KINGS II	107
ADVERSARIES	1	28	PHILIPPIANS	289
ADVERSITIES	10	19	SAMUEL I	86
AFFLICT	15	13	GENESIS	30
ALABASTER	26	7	MATTHEW	244
ALLOTTED	47	22	GENESIS	40
ALLOY	1	25	ISAIAH	169
ALLURE	6	25	PROVERBS	154
ALMS	11	41	LUKE	253
AMBUSH	8	4	JOSHUA	73
AMEND	35	15	JEREMIAH	184
AMISS	5	24	JOB	135
ANNUL	14	27	ISAIAH	172
APPAREL	1	24	SAMUEL II	98
APPEASE	32	20	GENESIS	35
AQUEDUCT	18	17	KINGS II	108
ARBITRATE	47	3	ISAIAH	175
ARRAY	20	30	JUDGES	80
ASCENDING	28	12	GENESIS	88
ASCRIBED	18	8	SAMUEL I	89
ASPS	140	3	PSALMS	149
ATONEMENT	29	33	EXODUS	49
ATTIRE	5	10	JUDGES	77
AVAILS	5	13	ESTHER	131
AVENGE	24	12	SAMUEL I	90
AWL	15	17	DEUTERONOMY	68
BEFALL	42	4	GENESIS	38
BEGUILING	2	14	PETER II	313
BEREAVED	27	45	GENESIS	33
BESIEGE	20	19	DEUTERONOMY	68
BETROTHED	22	16	EXODUS	48
BEVELED	6	4	KINGS I	100
BEWAILED	11	37	JUDGES	78
BILLOWS	2	3	JONAH	219
BLASPHEMED	24	11	LEVITICUS	57
BLEATING	15	14	SAMUEL I	88
BLIGHTED	41	23	GENESIS	37
BOUNTIFULLY	13	6	PSALMS	145
BRAMBLE	9	14	JUDGES	77

4

WORD LIST

WORD	CHAPTER	VERSE	BOOK	PAGE
BRANDISH	32	10	EZEKIEL	194
BRAY	6	5	JOB	135
BREACH	106	23	PSALMS	148
BRIDLE	19	28	KINGS II	109
BRIERS	5	6	ISAIAH	171
BROOD	1	4	ISAIAH	169
BULWARKS	48	13	PSALMS	146
BURNISHED	1	7	EZEKIEL	191
BUTTRESS	26	9	CHRONICLES II	117
CALAMITY	1	13	OBADIAH	215
CANOPIES	22	12	SAMUEL II	94
CARCASSES	15	11	GENESIS	30
CAROUSING	21	34	LUKE	253
CATASTROPHE	11	23	JEREMIAH	183
CAULDRON	2	14	SAMUEL I	85
CAVALRY	9	19	KINGS I	101
CENTURION	8	5	MATTHEW	243
CHAFF	21	18	JOB	138
CHASTENING	34	31	JOB	140
CHERUBIM	3	24	GENESIS	27
CHRONICLES	16	14	KINGS I	102
CIRCUMSPECT	23	13	EXODUS	49
CISTERN	11	36	LEVITICUS	56
CLAMOR	4	31	EPHESIANS	285
CLEFTS	30	6	JOB	138
CLOVEN	11	4	LEVITICUS	55
COMMEMORATE	16	4	CHRONICLES I	113
COMPELLED	13	12	SAMUEL I	87
COMPENSATE	7	4	ESTHER	131
COMPLACENCY	1	32	PROVERBS	153
COMPULSORY	1	8	ESTHER	131
CONCILIATION	10	4	ECCLESIASTES	159
CONCOURSES	1	21	PROVERBS	153
CONCUBINE	22	24	GENESIS	31
CONFEDERACY	1	7	OBADIAH	125
CONFISCATION	7	26	EZRA	123
CONFOUNDED	19	26	KINGS II	108
CONGEALED	15	8	EXODUS	47
CONSPIRED	37	18	GENESIS	36
CONSTITUENCY	12	5	KINGS II	107
CONSUMMATION	119	96	PSALMS	148
CONTEMPTIBLE	1	7	MALACHI	239
CONTENTIONS	2	9	TITUS	305
CONTINGENTS	11	7	KINGS II	107
CONTRITE	34	18	PSALMS	145
CONVEX	7	20	KINGS I	101
CONVOCATION	12	16	EXODUS	47
CORIANDER	16	31	EXODUS	47

WORD LIST

WORD	CHAPTER	VERSE	BOOK	PAGE
COUNTENANCE	4	5	GENESIS	28
COVENANT	9	11	GENESIS	28
COVETOUSNESS	18	21	EXODUS	47
CRAG	39	28	JOB	140
CUD	11	3	LEVITICUS	55
CURDS	7	15	ISAIAH	171
CURRENCY	23	16	GENESIS	32
DAPPLED	6	3	ZECHARIAH	235
DAUBED	2	3	EXODUS	45
DEBASES	7	7	ECCLESIASTES	159
DEFERRED	13	12	PROVERBS	154
DEFILE	34	5	GENESIS	35
DEGENERATE	2	21	JEREMIAH	181
DECEPTIVE	2	14	LAMENTATIONS	187
DENOUNCE	23	7	NUMBERS	62
DEPLETE	41	30	GENESIS	37
DEPLOY	4	6	JUDGES	77
DEPOSED	5	20	DANIEL	199
DERANGED	51	7	JEREMIAH	184
DERISION	44	13	PSALMS	146
DESCENDANTS	35	12	GENESIS	35
DESCENDING	28	12	GENESIS	33
DESOLATE	1	7	MICAH	223
DESTITUTE	6	5	TIMOTHY I	297
DIADEM	28	5	ISAIAH	173
DISCERN	3	9	KINGS I	100
DISCLOSE	49	4	PSALMS	146
DISCOURSE	27	1	JOB	138
DISDAINED	17	42	SAMUEL I	89
DISMAYED	45	3	GENESIS	39
DISPOSED	22	30	NUMBERS	62
DISSIPATION	1	6	TITUS	305
DISTRAUGHT	88	15	PSALMS	147
DIVINATION	44	5	GENESIS	39
DOCILE	11	19	JEREMIAH	182
DOE	5	19	PROVERBS	153
DOWRY	34	12	GENESIS	35
DRAGNET	1	15	HABAKKUK	231
DREGS	75	8	PSALMS	147
DROMEDARY	2	23	JEREMIAH	181
DROPSY	14	2	LUKE	253
DROSS	119	119	PSALMS	148
DROVES	32	16	GENESIS	35
EAVES	7	9	KINGS I	101
EDICT	6	11	EZRA	123
EDIFIES	14	4	CORINTHIANS	273
ELOQUENT	4	10	EXODUS	45

6

WORD LIST

WORD	CHAPTER	VERSE	BOOK	PAGE
EMASCULATED	23	1	DEUTERONOMY	69
EMBALM	50	2	GENESIS	41
EMBANKMENT	19	43	LUKE	253
EMINENT	11	5	CORINTHIANS II	277
EMITTED	38	9	GENESIS	36
ENCAMPMENT	42	27	GENESIS	38
ENDEARMENT	26	8	GENESIS	32
ENDOWMENT	30	20	GENESIS	34
ENDURE	1	6	NAHUM	227
ENIGMA	1	6	PROVERBS	153
ENMITY	3	15	GENESIS	27
ENTRAILS	29	13	EXODUS	49
ENVOYS	68	31	PSALMS	146
EPISTLE	5	9	CORINTHIANS I	273
ERRED	5	18	LEVITICUS	55
ESTRANGED	19	13	JOB	138
EUNUCHS	9	32	KINGS II	107
EWE	21	28	GENESIS	31
EXACTED	15	20	KINGS II	107
EXHORTED	11	7	JEREMIAH	182
EXPEDIENT	18	14	JOHN	257
EXPEDITION	23	13	SAMUEL I	89
EXTOLLED	66	17	PSALMS	146
EXTORTED	6	2	LEVITICUS	55
FALLOW	23	11	EXODUS	48
FALTER	18	21	KINGS I	102
FEEBLER	30	42	GENESIS	34
FERVOR	8	2	ZECHARIAH	235
FESTAL	3	21	ISAIAH	170
FETTERS	16	21	JUDGES	79
FIDELITY	2	10	TITUS	305
FILLY	1	9	SONG OF SOLOMON	163
FIRMAMENT	1	6	GENESIS	27
FLANGES	7	35	KINGS I	101
FLAX	9	31	EXODUS	46
FOAL	9	9	ZECHARIAH	235
FODDER	19	19	JUDGES	79
FOLIAGE	19	11	EZEKIEL	192
FOLLY	85	8	PSALMS	147
FORDS	12	5	JUDGES	78
FORNICATION	23	17	ISAIAH	173
FURROWS	31	38	JOB	139
FUTILE	1	21	ROMANS	267
GALL	16	13	JOB	137
GARRISON	13	3	SAMUEL I	87
GAUNT	41	3	GENESIS	36
GENEALOGY	5	1	GENESIS	28
GIRDED	8	13	GENESIS	55

WORD LIST

WORD	CHAPTER	VERSE	BOOK	PAGE
GLEANINGS	19	9	LEVITICUS	56
GLUTTON	21	20	DEUTERONOMY	68
GNASHES	16	9	JOB	137
GOADS	26	14	ACTS	262
GOBLET	7	2	SONG OF SOLOMON	163
GROVES	8	14	SAMUEL I	86
GULLIBLE	3	6	TIMOTHY II	301
HALLOW	28	38	EXODUS	49
HAUGHTY	101	5	PSALMS	147
HAVOC	8	3	ACTS	261
HEARTH	36	23	JEREMIAH	184
HEDGE	1	10	JOB	135
HEED	39	10	GENESIS	36
HINDER	24	56	GENESIS	32
HOE	7	25	ISAIAH	171
HOISTED	27	40	ACTS	263
HOMAGE	1	31	KINGS I	99
HORDE	23	24	EZEKIEL	193
HYPOCRITE	8	13	JOB	136
IMPLEMENTS	9	29	CHRONICLES I	113
IMPLORE	5	7	MARK	249
IMPUDENT	2	4	EZEKIEL	191
IMPUTED	17	4	LEVITICUS	56
INCITED	4	15	EZRA	123
INDIGNANT	4	1	NEHEMIAH	127
INDUCED	14	9	EZEKIEL	192
INIQUITY	15	16	GENESIS	30
INLETS	5	17	JUDGES	77
INSOLENCE	17	28	SAMUEL I	88
INSUBORDINATE	1	9	TIMOTHY I	297
INTERCESSOR	59	16	ISAIAH	176
INTOXICATING	1	15	SAMUEL I	85
ITINERANT	19	13	ACTS	261
JAVELIN	25	7	NUMBERS	62
JEERING	29	8	CHRONICLES II	118
JOSTLE	2	4	NAHUM	227
JURISDICTION	23	7	LUKE	254
KINDLE	9	18	ISAIAH	171
LANCES	18	28	KINGS I	102
LANGUISHED	47	13	GENESIS	40
LATTICE	7	17	KINGS I	101
LAUD	117	1	PSALMS	148
LAVER	30	18	EXODUS	50
LENTILS	25	34	GENESIS	32
LEVIATHAN	3	8	JOB	135
LEVY	31	28	NUMBERS	63
LEWDNESS	20	6	JUDGES	79
LICENTIOUSNESS	12	21	CORINTHIANS II	277

8

WORD LIST

WORD	CHAPTER	VERSE	BOOK	PAGE
LINEAGE	19	32	GENESIS	30
LINTEL	12	7	EXODUS	46
LOATHE	7	18	EXODUS	46
LULLED	16	19	JUDGES	78
LYE	2	22	JEREMIAH	181
MAGISTRATES	7	25	EZRA	123
MALADY	16	12	CHRONICLES II	117
MALICIOUS	2	8	KINGS I	99
MALIGN	30	10	PROVERBS	154
MAMMON	6	24	MATTHEW	243
MANDRAKES	30	14	GENESIS	34
MANIFOLD	9	19	NEHEMIAH	127
MANTLE	28	14	SAMUEL I	90
MARINER	27	29	EZEKIEL	193
MARROW	21	24	JOB	138
MARSH	8	11	JOB	136
MASONS	5	11	SAMUEL II	93
MAST	27	5	EZEKIEL	193
MATRIX	49	1	ISAIAH	175
MEEK	5	5	MATTHEW	243
MERCENARIES	46	21	JEREMIAH	184
MILLET	4	9	EZEKIEL	191
MIRE	30	19	JOB	139
MORTAR	27	22	PROVERBS	155
MUSE	143	5	PSALMS	149
MUSTERED	8	10	JOSHUA	73
MYRIADS	21	20	ACTS	262
NATIVITY	21	30	EZEKIEL	192
NETTLES	9	6	HOSEA	203
OBSCURE	33	19	ISAIAH	174
OBSTINATE	2	30	DEUTERONOMY	67
ORDAINED	1	5	JEREMIAH	181
ORDINANCE	12	14	EXODUS	47
PAGAN	10	10	EZRA	124
PALATE	34	3	JOB	140
PAPYRUS	8	11	JOB	136
PARABLES	20	49	EZEKIEL	192
PARAMOURS	23	20	EZEKIEL	192
PARAPET	22	8	DEUTERONOMY	68
PARCHED	23	14	LEVITICUS	57
PARTITION	40	3	EXODUS	50
PATRIARCHS	7	8	ACTS	261
PAVILION	27	5	PSALMS	145
PEDDLING	2	17	CORINTHIANS II	277
PENITENTS	1	27	ISAIAH	169
PURGATORY	17	12	JOHN	257
PERPETUAL	9	12	GENESIS	29
PESTILENCE	5	3	EXODUS	45

WORD LIST

WORD	CHAPTER	VERSE	BOOK	PAGE
PESTLE	27	22	PROVERBS	155
PHILISTINES	14	1	JUDGES	78
PHYLACTERIES	23	5	MATTHEW	244
PILFERING	2	10	TITUS	305
PILGRIMAGE	47	9	GENESIS	40
PILLAGE	29	19	EZEKIEL	193
PINNACLES	54	12	ISAIAH	176
PLAGUES	12	17	GENESIS	29
PLATITUDES	13	12	JOB	137
PLOWSHARES	13	21	SAMUEL I	87
PLUMB	7	7	AMOS	211
PLUMMET	21	13	KINGS II	109
PLUNDER	3	22	EXODUS	45
POMEGRANATE	39	24	EXODUS	50
POMP	5	14	ISAIAH	171
PORTICO	7	6	KINGS I	100
POSTERITY	21	23	GENESIS	31
POULTICE	38	21	ISAIAH	174
PRATING	10	10	PROVERBS	154
PRECEPT	10	5	MARK	249
PREEMINENCE	1	18	COLOSSIANS	293
PREMEDITATION	21	14	EXODUS	48
PRESUMPTUOUSLY	15	30	NUMBERS	61
PRINCIPALITIES	6	12	EPHESIANS	285
PROCONSUL	13	7	ACTS	261
PRODIGAL	15	13	LUKE	253
PROFANING	2	10	MALACHI	239
PROGNOSTICATORS	47	13	ISAIAH	175
PROMINENT	1	42	KINGS I	99
PROPITIATION	3	25	ROMANS	267
PROSELYTE	23	15	MATTHEW	244
PROSTRATED	43	28	GENESIS	39
PROVISIONS	14	11	GENESIS	29
PRUDENT	5	13	AMOS	211
PURGE	1	25	ISAIAH	169
PUTREFY	10	1	ECCLESIASTES	159
PYRE	30	33	ISAIAH	173
QUARRY	5	17	KINGS I	100
RABBLE	30	12	JOB	139
RAMPART	20	15	SAMUEL II	94
RATIONS	47	22	GENESIS	40
RAVENOUS	7	15	MATTHEW	243
RAVINE	2	36	DEUTERONOMY	67
RAVISHED	20	5	JUDGES	79
RAZE	137	7	PSALMS	149
REALM	6	3	DANIEL	199
REBUKE	4	2	TIMOTHY II	301
RECESSES	24	3	SAMUEL I	90

WORD LIST

WORD	CHAPTER	VERSE	BOOK	PAGE
RECONCILE	1	20	COLOSSIANS	293
RELENT	3	9	JONAH	219
REMISSION	26	28	MATTHEW	244
REMNANT	1	9	ISAIAH	169
RENOWN	16	2	NUMBERS	62
REPRISAL	1	15	OBADIAH	215
REPROACH	30	23	GENESIS	34
REPROOFS	6	23	PROVERBS	154
REPROVE	20	16	GENESIS	31
RESERVOIR	22	11	ISAIAH	172
RESTITUTION	5	7	NUMBERS	61
RETINUE	10	'2	KINGS I	102
RETRIBUTION	6	23	CHRONICLES II	117
REVILE	22	28	EXODUS	48
REVILING	2	11	PETER II	313
RIFLED	14	2	ZECHARIAH	236
RIGOR	1	13	EXODUS	45
RIVULETS	31	4	EZEKIEL	194
ROGUE	16	7	SAMUEL II	93
RUDDY	16	12	SAMUEL I	88
SANCTIFIED	2	3	GENESIS	27
SATIATE	31	14	JEREMIAH	183
SATRAPS	8	36	EZRA	124
SAVORY	27	4	GENESIS	33
SCARCITY	8	9	DEUTERONOMY	67
SCEPTER	49	10	GENESIS	41
SCHISM	12	25	CORINTHIANS I	273
SCOFF	1	10	HABAKKUK	231
SCOURGING	19	20	LEVITICUS	56
SCRIBE	18	18	KINGS II	108
SCRUPLES	15	1	ROMANS	267
SECLUSION	20	3	SAMUEL II	93
SEDITION	4	15	EZRA	123
SELVEDGE	26	4	EXODUS	49
SEPULCHER	22	16	ISAIAH	173
SEVER	2	22	ISAIAH	170
SHEAF	37	7	GENESIS	36
SHEATH	17	51	SAMUEL I	89
SICKLE	16	9	DEUTERONOMY	68
SIGNET	41	42	GENESIS	37
SIMILITUDE	3	9	JAMES	309
SINEWS	10	11	JOB	137
SINGED	3	27	DANIEL	199
SKIFF	27	30	ACTS	262
SKIRTED	2	1	DEUTERONOMY	67
SLUGGARD	6	6	PROVERBS	153
SNEER	1	13	MALACHI	239
SOJOURNED	20	9	JOSHUA	73

WORD LIST

WORD	CHAPTER	VERSE	BOOK	PAGE
SOVEREIGNTY	14	47	SAMUEL I	87
SPAN	40	12	ISAIAH	174
SPELT	9	32	EXODUS	46
STAG	8	14	SONG OF SOLOMON	164
STATURE	16	7	SAMUEL I	88
STEADFAST	6	26	DANIEL	199
STEALTH	2	4	GALATIANS	281
STEWARD	43	16	GENESIS	39
STRIFE	13	7	GENESIS	29
STUPOR	11	8	ROMANS	267
SUBSIDED	8	1	GENESIS	28
SUBVERT	8	3	JOB	135
SUCCULENT	33	20	JOB	139
SUCKLING	7	9	SAMUEL I	86
SULLEN	20	43	KINGS I	103
SUMPTUOUS	1	16	HABAKKUK	231
SUPERFLUOUS	9	1	CORINTHIANS II	277
SUPPLANT	9	4	JEREMIAH	182
SUPPLICATION	12	10	ZECHARIAH	235
SURETY	43	9	GENESIS	38
SUSTENANCE	6	4	JUDGES	77
SWADDLING	38	9	JOB	140
TABERNACLE	33	7	EXODUS	50
TARRY	45	9	GENESIS	40
TAUNT	24	9	JEREMIAH	183
TEMPEST	9	17	JOB	136
TEMPESTUOUS	1	11	JONAH	219
THRESHOLD	5	4	SAMUEL I	86
TIMBREL	31	27	GENESIS	34
TINDER	1	31	ISAIAH	170
TITHE	14	20	GENESIS	30
TOIL	41	51	GENESIS	37
TORRENTS	14	19	JOB	137
TRANSFIGURED	17	2	MATTHEW	244
TRANSGRESSION	14	18	NUMBERS	61
TRAVERSING	27	19	EZEKIEL	193
TREATY	3	1	KINGS I	99
TRENCH	18	32	KINGS I	103
TRIBULATION	26	24	SAMUEL I	90
TROUGH	24	20	GENESIS	32
TRUDGING	2	7	DEUTERONOMY	67
TUMULT	24	17	NUMBERS	62
TUNIC	3	21	GENESIS	27
TURMOIL	15	5	CHRONICLES II	117
TURNCOAT	2	4	MICAH	223
UNDULY	5	20	ECCLESIASTES	159
UNTEMPERED	13	10	EZEKIEL	192

WORD LIST

WORD	CHAPTER	VERSE	BOOK	PAGE
VAGABOND	4	12	GENESIS	28
VALIANT	10	26	SAMUEL I	86
VANQUISH	32	13	JOB	139
VASSAL	17	3	KINGS II	108
VEHEMENT	8	6	SONG OF SOLOMON	163
VERDURE	6	11	SONG OF SOLOMON	163
VERIFIED	42	20	GENESIS	38
VERMILION	22	14	JEREMIAH	183
VESTIBULE	6	3	KINGS I	100
VEXED	16	16	JUDGES	78
VIGOR	10	8	DANIEL	199
VILE	3	13	SAMUEL I	85
VINDICATION	17	2	PSALMS	145
VIPER	49	17	GENESIS	41
VISAGE	52	14	ISAIAH	175
WAIFS	5	3	LAMENTATIONS	187
WAIL	16	7	ISAIAH	172
WALLOWED	20	12	SAMUEL II	93
WANE	17	4	ISAIAH	172
WANTON	3	16	ISAIAH	170
WARES	10	31	NEHEMIAH	127
WEANED	1	22	SAMUEL I	85
WEARIED	2	17	MALACHI	239
WICK	43	17	ISAIAH	174
WILES	6	11	EPHESIANS	285
WINNOWING	3	12	MATTHEW	243
WOE	4	7	SAMUEL I	85
WRESTED	11	23	CHRONICLES I	113
WRITHE	2	6	JOEL	207
YOKE	10	27	ISAIAH	172
YONDER	22	5	GENESIS	31
ZEALOUS	11	29	NUMBERS	61

TABLE OF CONTENTS

INTRODUCTION	i	AMOS	209
GENESIS	25	OBADIAH	213
EXODUS	43	JONAH	217
LEVITICUS	53	MICAH	221
NUMBERS	59	NAHUM	225
DEUTERONOMY	65	HABAKKUK	229
JOSHUA	71	ZECHARIAH	233
JUDGES	75	MALACHI	237
SAMUEL I	83	MATTHEW	241
SAMUEL II	91	MARK	247
KINGS I	97	LUKE	251
KINGS II	105	JOHN	255
CHRONICLES I	111	ACTS	259
CHRONICLES II	115	ROMANS	265
EZRA	121	CORINTHIANS I	271
NEHEMIAH	125	CORINTHIANS II	275
ESTHER	129	GALATIANS	279
JOB	133	EPHESIANS	283
PSALMS	143	PHILIPPIANS	287
PROVERBS	151	COLOSSIANS	291
ECCLESIASTES	157	TIMOTHY I	295
SONG OF SOLOMON	161	TIMOTHY II	299
ISAIAH	167	TITUS	303
JEREMIAH	179	JAMES	307
LAMENTATIONS	185	PETER II	311
EZEKIEL	189	Rooted In The Word (Roots and Affixes)	315
DANIEL	197		
HOSEA	201	Answers to Random Review	321
JOEL	205	Answers to "Try These"	327

Other Books By Eugene Williams, Sr.

GETTING THE JOB YOU WANT WITH THE AUDIOVISUAL PORTFOLIO

KEYS TO QUICK WRITING SKILLS: SENTENCE COMBINING AND TEXT RECONSTRUCTION

BLUEPRINT FOR EDUCATIONAL CHANGE: IMPROVING REASONING, LITERACIES AND SCIENCE ACHIEVEMENT WITH COOPERATIVE LEARNING

IT'S A READING THING: HELP YOUR CHILD UNDERSTAND: PARENT'S GUIDE TO IMPROVING STUDENTS' VERBAL PERFORMANCE ON STANDARDIZED EXAMINATIONS LIKE THE PSAT AND SAT

Other Books By Eugene Williams, Jr.

REFLECTIONS OF A CONFUSED MIDDLE CLASS BLACK YOUTH

THE "RAISIN-IN-MILK" SYNDROME: TEN SURVIVAL TIPS FOR BLACK STUDENTS AT PREDOMINANTLY WHITE COLLEGES AND UNIVERSITIES

IT'S A READING THING: HELP YOUR CHILD UNDERSTAND: PARENT'S GUIDE TO IMPROVING STUDENTS' VERBAL PERFORMANCE ON STANDARDIZED EXAMINATIONS LIKE THE PSAT AND SAT

Published Poems

"RAISIN-IN-MILK"

"AFRAID OF US"

"I HEAR YOU, LANGSTON"

"RESPECT"

AT WATER'S EDGE (Anthology)- The National Library of Poetry

INTRODUCTION

For the last thirteen years, we have been involved in informing parents, teachers, and students throughout the United States about materials and practices to use to improve verbal scores on standardized examinations like the PSAT and the SAT. In most of our information and training sessions, we have told the participants that the Bible is rich with words found on these examinations and that they should use the Bible as one source for enriching their vocabularies and improving their scores. While we informed them of the Bible as a good vocabulary source, we did not provide them a list of words that we thought they should know in order to understand the Bible or to improve their vocabularies. This concerned us a great deal. Obsessed with the idea that God wanted a guide developed with the list of words to be shared with students, teachers, parents, and Christian educators, we developed this guide. Thus, we now have a vocabulary list of 464 words found in the <u>Ever Increasing Faith Study Bible</u> and <u>The Possibility Thinkers Bible</u> (The New King James Version). The list includes words that, based on our survey with students and adults, some people may have difficulty understanding. Some of them are words found on examinations like the PSAT and the SAT; others are words with which many high school students and some adults are not familiar. The list has been reviewed and duplicate words with like roots have been eliminated. Because of the use of alternative spellings in the <u>Ever Increasing Faith Study Bible</u>, the spellings of some of the words have been changed to those more commonly in use.

This guide can be used by elementary and high school students as well as adults who wish to improve their vocabularies. It can be used as a separate text or a supplementary textbook by English teachers, SAT verbal instructors, and Christian educators. When using it, the reader might want to read the chapters in the Bible from which the verses come so as to acquire a full understanding of the Biblical message. One other way that the reader may get the full understanding of the verses and chapters is to read guides to the Bible, like THE COMPACT SURVEY OF THE BIBLE by John Balchin, general editor. But remember, that the purpose is not to teach scripture but to enhance one's vocabulary while inspiring students to study the teachings found in the Bible. The Bible, read by more people than any other book, is an excellent vocabulary source. Make use of it: Become "grounded in the word."

Enjoy this, our first attempt, to help you learn words in context from the Bible.

Eugene Williams, Sr.

Eugene Williams, Jr.

TO THE ADULT

Reading the BIBLE with understanding should be the goal of every Christian. This goal is enhanced when the reader knows the meaning of unfamiliar words found in the BIBLE.

GROUNDED IN THE WORD is designed solely to increase the reader's knowledge of words-words that may present the reader from fully comprehending the scripture. With this increased knowledge, the adult is better equipped to help others, adults and children, understand and appreciate the word of God.

Parents

What better source could you use than the BIBLE to introduce your child to new words like <u>enigma</u>, <u>enmity</u>, <u>iniquity</u>, and <u>obstinate</u>? These words and many others in this guide have appeared on standardized examinations like the PSAT and the SAT. They appear in some of our great pieces of literature and in newspaper and magazine articles. Seeing these words in biblical scripture, knowing their definitions, synonyms, and parts of speech, your child will become stronger verbally.

As you introduce your child to the words in this guide, talk about the importance of the BIBLE. Make your child cognizant of the fact that our beliefs should be determined by the messages of the Bible and that our behavior should be shaped by the word of God.

Some suggestions for making the study of words in this guide interesting and enjoyable include the following: (1) Provide your child information on the background of each chapter. (2) Read the bible verse aloud to the child, then ask what word is an unfamiliar one. (3) Provide the definition, then read the sentence from the guide with the new word. (4) Present some of the synonyms to the child encouraging him/her to look up their definitions. (5) Encourage your child to use newly learned words in sentences. This indicates whether the word is really learned.

You or your child may also make flash cards, pieces of paper, cardboard, or index cards, with the word on one side and the definition on the other side. If there are bible verses in this guide that you want your child to memorize for any special reason, you may place the verse on one side of the flash card also. Make this activity a fun game.

Teacher

GROUNDED IN THE WORD may be used as the main vocabulary guide for your students or as a supplementary vocabulary building manual. The Word List found in the beginning section of this guide provides a quick overview of the words to which the reader will be exposed. Using this Word List, you may begin teaching these words by developing and administering a diagnostic vocabulary test to ascertain how many of the words your students know. This diagnostic activity can be simply a list of the words requiring the students to indicate by a check of yes or no whether they know the definition of each word.

Since every book of the BIBLE is not included in this guide, you may begin your first lesson with Genesis or you may begin with chapters in which you or your students may be most interested based on previous biblical study.

If you feel that your students need background information on the chapters in this guide, consider providing them that information using references like THE COMPACT SURVEY OF THE BIBLE, published by Bethany House Publishers of Minneapolis, Minnesota.

In introducing your students to the words in this guide, read aloud each bible verse emphasizing the pronunciation of each underlined word. To make sure that the students can pronounce the words, encourage them to repeat after you the correct pronunciation of the words. Do the same for the synonyms for each word.

Encourage your students to keep a vocabulary notebook. In this notebook, the students should include the vocabulary words and their synonyms used in sentences. This activity would help students to build an extensive vocabulary.

Use the Random Review and Try These exercises as you would like to with your students. But create your own exercises to test the students knowledge and use of the vocabulary words and their synonyms.

Learning new words can be a fun activity. Make it such.

TO THE STUDENT

Did you know that there were so many unfamiliar words in the BIBLE even words that you may see on standardized examinations like the ones you take in school and for college admission?

Using GROUNDED IN THE WORD, you can increase your vocabulary, enhance your writing and speaking skills, and expand your knowledge of the BIBLE. While this guide is not designed to make you a better biblical student, it may motivate you to develop an appreciation and better understanding for words found in scripture. It may even inspire you to read the BIBLE more seriously to understand the historical and literary aspects of the BIBLE. If you wish to gain a greater understanding of the background of the scripture from which the words are taken, use reference guides like THE COMPACT SURVEY OF THE BIBLE. It's a handy reference book which gives an introduction, an outline, the main message, applications, and key themes for each book of the BIBLE.

As you study each word, pay special attention to its meaning, synonyms, part of speech, and the sentence in which the word is used. Use your dictionary for the pronunciation of the words.

One excellent and enjoyable way to enhance the acquisition of the meaning of the words is to make flash cards, placing the word on one side and the definition accompanied by the corresponding bible verse on the other side. With these cards, you can study the words with a classmate or a family member.

To gain a better understanding of those synonyms in the guide that are new to you, look up their meanings in your dictionary. Then, try using them in sentences.

The <u>Random Review</u> and <u>Try These</u> exercises test your understanding of the words. Complete these as soon as you think you know the definitions of words in each chapter. Become more rooted in the word by reviewing the words in the Rooted In The Word section.

ACKNOWLEDGEMENT

TO

- GOD FOR THE INSPIRATION TO INITIATE AND COMPLETE THIS GUIDE

- Dr. Mary H. Johnson, a very special Christian wife and mother

- Mr. Malcolm Brown, a very special young man who provided assistance in organizing this guide

- Ms. Mardi Pinkney, a talented young Christian lady for her special support

**DEDICATED
TO
ALL PEOPLE WHO LOVE
TO READ THE BIBLE**

Word List

GENESIS

GENESIS
1:6
Then God said "Let there be a <u>firmament</u> in the midst of the waters, and let it divide the waters from the waters."
Definition: sky
Synonyms: empyrean, heavens, welkin
noun: firmament
adjective: firmamental
Pilots spend a considerable amount of time in the **firmament**.
2:3
Then God blessed the seventh day and <u>sanctified</u> it, because in it He rested from all His work which God had created and made.
Definition: make holy
Synonyms: holy, blessed, consecrated, hallowed, sacred
noun: sanctification, sanctifier
verb: sanctify
Born again Christians are often regarded as **sanctified** people.
3:15
And I will put <u>enmity</u> Between you and the woman, And between your seed and her seed; He shall bruise your head, And you shall bruise his heel.
Definition: mutual hatred
Synonyms: animosity, animus, antagonism, antipathy, hostility, rancor
noun: enmity
Adolf Hitler displayed a great deal of **enmity** towards Jews.
3:21
Also for Adam and his wife the LORD God made <u>tunics</u> of skin and clothed them.
Definition: ancient knee-length garment, hip-length blouse, or jacket
noun: tunic
Scottish kilts are **tunics**.
3:24
So He drove out the man; and He placed <u>cherubim</u> at the east of the garden of Eden, and a flaming sword which turned every way, to guard the way to the tree of life.
Definition: angel, chubby child
noun: cherub
adjective: cherubic
adverb: cherubically
The **cherubim** are messengers of God.
4:5
But He did not respect Cain and his offering. And Cain was very angry, and

his <u>countenance</u> fell.
Definition: face or facial expression
Synonyms: look, cast, expression, face, visage
noun: countenance
The smiling baby had a happy **countenance**.
    4:12
When you till the ground it shall no longer yield its strength to you. A fugitive and a <u>vagabond</u> you shall be on the earth.
Definition: wanderer with no home
Synonyms: itinerant, ambulant, ambulatory, nomadic, per ambulatory, peripatetic, roving, vagrant, wandering, bum, canter, derelict, drifter, floater, hobo, piker, roadster, tramp, vagrant, weary willie
noun: vagabond, vagabondism
adjective: vagabondish
Bohemians and Gypsies are two kinds of **vagabonds**.
    5:1
This is the book of the <u>genealogy</u> of Adam. In the day that God created man. He made him in the likeness of God.
Definition: study of family pedigrees
Synonyms: family tree, pedigree
noun: genealogy, genealogist
adjective: genealogical
verb: genealogically
<u>Roots</u> is a novel about Alex Haley's **genealogy**.
    8:1
Then God remembered Noah, and every living thing, and all the animals that were with him in the ark. And God made a wind to pass over the earth, and the waters <u>subsided.</u>
Definition: die down in intensity
Synonyms: abated, ebbed, lulled, moderated, relented, slackened, waned
noun: subsidence
verb: subside
Once it stopped snowing, the weatherman said the blizzard had **subsided**.
    9:11
Thus I establish My <u>covenant</u> with you : Never again shall all flesh be cut off by the waters of the flood; never again shall there be a flood to destroy the earth.
Definition: agreement
Synonyms: contract, bond, compact, pact, transaction, vow, pledge
noun: covenant, covenanter

adjective: covenantal
verb: covenant
A contract is a written **covenant** between two people.
    9:12
And God said: This is the sign of the covenant which I make between Me and you, and every living creature that is with you, for <u>perpetual</u> generations.
Definition: continuing forever, occurring continually
Synonyms: continual, ceaseless, constant, endless, continuous, everlasting, incessant, interminable, minutely timeless, unceasing, interrupted, unremitting
noun: perpetuity
adjective: perpetual
adverb: perpetually
Throughout American history, there has been a **perpetual** struggle for equality among the races.
    12:17
But the LORD plagued Pharaoh and his house with great <u>plagues</u> because of Sarah, Abram's wife.
Definition: scourge, contagious disease, divine punishment
Synonyms: troublesome, calamity, misfortune
noun: plague
verb: plague
At some point in our lives, we have all been **plagued** with a problem.
    13:7
And there was <u>strife</u> between the herdsmen of Abram's livestock and the herdsmen of Lot's livestock. The Canaanites and the Perizzites then dwelt in the land.
Definition: conflict
Synonyms: discord, contention, difference, disharmony, dissension, dissent, dissidence, dissonance
noun: strife
adjective: strifeless
Strife between a husband and wife often leads to divorce.
    14:11
Then God took all the goods of Sodom and Gomorrah, and all their <u>provisions</u>, and went their way.
Definition: something provided, stock of food, a clause
noun: provision, provisioners
verb: provisioned, provisioning
Before a major snowstorm occurs, go to the store for **provisions**.
    14:20
And blessed be God Most High Who has delivered your enemies into your

hand. And he gave him a tithe of all.
Definition: tenth part or given especially for the support of a church
noun: tithe, tither
verb: tithe
We **tithe** when we donate 10% of our earnings to a church.

15:11
And when the vultures came down on the carcasses, Abram drove them away.
Definition: dead body of animal, worthless remains
Synonyms: cadaver, corpse, remains, shell
noun: carcass
The lions killed the gazelles, ate them, and left their **carcasses** for the vultures to eat.

15:13
And then he said to Abram, Know certainly that your descendants, will be strangers in a land that is not theirs, and will serve them, and the will afflict them four hundred years.
Definition: cause pain and distress to
Synonyms: agonize, crucify, excruciate, marrow, martyr, martyrize, rack, smite, strike, torment, torture, try, wrong
noun: affliction
adjective: afflictive
verb: afflict
adverb: afflictively
Some cures can **afflict** the patient more than the disease.

15:16
But in the fourth generation they shall return here, for the iniquity of Amorites is not yet complete.
Definition: wickedness
Synonyms: evil, crime, tort, wrong, wrongdoing
noun: iniquity, iniquitousness
adjective: iniquitous
adverb:iniquitously
The people of Sodom and Gomorrah were destroyed because of their **iniquities**.

19:32
Come, let us make our father drink wine, and we will lie with him, that we may preserve the lineage of our father.
Definition: descent, from a common ancestor
Synonyms: ancestry, blood, descent, extraction, origin, pedigree, family, clan, folk, house, kin, race, stock, tribe

noun: lineage
An intensive review of birth records can reveal **lineage** of past centuries.

    20:16

Then to Sarah he said, "Behold, I have given to your brother a thousand pieces of silver; indeed this vindicates you before all who are with you and before others." Thus she was <u>reproved</u>.
Definition: express disapproval, find fault
Synonyms: rebuke, censure
noun: reprover
verb: reprove
adverb: reprovingly
Your mother will not hesitate to **reprove** you should you embarrass her publicly.

    21:23

Now therefore, swear to me by God that you will not deal falsely with me, with my offspring, or with my <u>posterity</u>: but that according to the kindness that I have done to you, you will do and to the land in which you have sojourned.
Definition: succeeding, generations
Synonyms: offspring, brood, children, descendants, issue, progeny, scions, seed
noun: posterity
John Rockefeller amassed a fortune and left it for his **posterity**.

    21:28

And Abraham set seven <u>ewe</u> lambs of the flock by themselves.
Definition: female sheep
noun: ewe
In ancient times, worshippers often sacrificed **ewes** to appease their gods.

    22:5

And Abraham said to his young man, "Stay here with the donkey; the lad and I will go <u>yonder</u> and worship and we will come back to you."
Definition: at or to that place; distant
Synonyms: beyond, farther, further
adjective: yonder
adverb: yonder
Stricken with wanderlust, the merchant marine travelled hither and yonder before finding a place to call home.

    22:24

His <u>concubine</u>, whose name was Reumah, also bore Tebah, Graham, Thahash, and Maachah.
Definition: mistress

noun: mistress
Monarchs of ancient kingdoms frequently retained the services of **concubines**.

23:16
And Abraham listened to Ephron; and Abraham weighed out the silver for Ephron which he had named in the hearing of the sons of Heth, four hundred shekels of silver, <u>currency</u> of the merchants.
Definition: nation's money in circulation
noun: currency
The **currency** of most nations has much less value than that of the United States.

24:20
Then she hastened and emptied her pitcher into the <u>trough</u>, ran back to the well to draw water, and drew for all his camels.
Definition: narrow container for animal feed or water
noun: trough
The children devoured the birthday cake like pigs at the **trough**.

24:56
And he said to them, Do not <u>hinder</u> me, since the LORD has prospered my way; send me away so that I may to my master.
Definition: obstruct or hold back
Synonyms: bar, block, brake, dam, impede, obstruct
noun: hinderer, hindrance
verb: hinder
My failing grade in mathematics **hindered** my graduation.

25:34
And Jacob gave Esau bread and stew of <u>lentils</u>; then he ate and drank, arose and went this way. Thus Esau despised his birthright.
Definition: small, edible seeds of a pea plant
noun: lentil
A bowl of **lentils** is always nourishing.

26:8
Now when it came to pass, when he had been there a long time, that Abimelech king of the Philistines look through a window, and saw, and there was Isaac showing <u>endearment</u> to Rebekah his wife.
Definition: make dear
noun: endearment
verb: endear
adverb: endearingly
The enthusiasm of children is their most **endearing** quality.

27:4
"And make me <u>savory</u> food, such as I love, and bring it to me that I may eat, that my soul may bless you before I die."
Definition: special flavor
Synonyms: palatable, appetizing, flavorsome, relishing, sapid, savorous, tasteful, tasty, toothsome, toothy
noun: savor, savoriness
adjective: savory, savorless, savorous
verb: savor
adverb: savorily
The **savory** aroma of the roast beef made my stomach growl.

27:45
Until your brother's anger turns away from you, and he forgets what you have done to him; then I will send and bring you from there. Why should I be <u>bereaved</u> also of you both in one day?
Definition: suffering the death of a loved one
Synonyms: bereft
noun: bereaved , bereavement
adjective: bereaved
verb: bereave
Following the death of their parents, the children were **bereaved** for months.

28:12
Then he dreamed, and behold, a ladder was set up on the earth, and its top reached to heaven; and there the angel of God were<u> ascending</u> and <u>descending</u> on it.
Definition: move upward
Synonyms:climbing, escalating, mounting, scaling
noun: ascension
adjective: ascendable, ascendible
verb: ascend
Since the elevator was temporarily inoperable, we were forced to **ascend** numerous stairwells.
Definition: move downward
Synonyms: lowering
noun: descent
adjective: descendant, descendent
verb: descend
Witnessing the cruel murder of his parents was the beginning of his **descent** into madness.

30:14
Now Reuben went in the days of wheat harvest and found mandrakes in the

field and brought them to his mother Leah. Then Rachel said to Leah, Please give me some of your son's <u>mandrakes.</u>
Definition: herb with a large forked root
noun: mandrake
The destitute family was reduced to selling **mandrakes** at the market.
    30:20
And Leah said, God has endowed me with a good <u>endowment;</u> now my husband will dwell with me, because I have borne him six sons. So she called his name Zebulun.
Definition: furnish with funds, furnish naturally
Synonyms: gift, present
noun: endowment
verb: endow
Wealthy alumni often present large **endowments** to universities.
    30:23
And she conceived and bore a son, and said, "God has taken away my <u>reproach</u>."
Definition: disgrace, rebuke
Synonyms: admonishment, admonition, chiding, rap, reprimand, reproof
noun: reproach, reproachfulness
adjective: reproachful
verb: reproach
adverb: reproachfully
An unruly student forced the teacher to publicly **reproach** her.
    30:42
But when the flocks were feeble, he did not put them in; so the <u>feebler</u> were Laban's and the stronger Jacob's.
Definition: weak, ineffective
Synonyms: decrepit, flimsy, fragile, frail, infirm, insubstantial, puny, unsound, weakly
noun: feebleness, feeblemindedness
adjective: feeble, feebleminded
adverb: feebly, feeblemindedly
Feebleness of mind and body is the result of aging.
    31:27
"Why did you flee away secretly, and steal away from me, and not tell me; for I might have sent you away with joy and songs, with <u>timbrel</u> and harp.
Definition: ancient type of tambourine
noun: timbrel
The archaeologist discovered several **timbrels** at her digging site.
    32:16

Then he delivered them to the hand of his servants, every drove by itself, and said to his servants, Pass over before me, and put some distance between successive **droves.**
Definition: crowd of moving people or animals
Synonyms: crowds, crushes, throngs, flocks, herds
noun: drove
During times of economic recession or depression, people migrate across borders in **droves.**
    32:20
And also say, Behold, your servant Jacob is behind us. For he said, I will **appease** him with the present that goes before me, and after I will see his face; perhaps he will accept me.
Definition: pacify with concessions
Synonyms: assuage, conciliate, mollify, placate, propitiate, sweeten, satisfy, content, gratify
noun: appeasement, appeaser
adjective: appeasable
verb: appease
Intransigent people simply refuse to be **appeased.**
    34:5
And Jacob heard that he had **defiled** Dinah his daughter. Now his sons were with his livestock in the field; so Jacob held his peace until they came.
Definition: make filthy or corrupt, profane or dishonor
Synonyms: impure, common, desecrated, polluted, profaned, unclean, soiled, tainted
noun: defilement, defiler
verb: defile
Defiling a church or a grave is considered a serious offense.
    34:12
Ask me ever so much **dowry** and gift, and I will give according to what you say to me; but give me the young woman as my wife.
Definition: property a woman gives her husband in marriage
Synonyms: dot, dower, marriage portion
noun: dowry
In some villages **dowries** are still required for a woman to be married.
    35:12
The land which I gave Abraham and Isaac I give to you; and to your **descendants** after you I give this land.
Definition: children
Synonyms: offspring, progeny
noun: descendant, descendent

A trust is an effective method a leaving money or property to **descendants**.
  37:7
"There we were, binding <u>sheaves</u> in the field. Then behold, my sheaf arose and also stood upright; and indeed your sheaves stood all around and bowed down to my sheaf."
Definition: bundle, especially grain stalks
noun: sheaf
Migrant laborers collected **sheaves** for transport to market.
  37:18
Now when they saw him afar off, even before he came near them, they <u>conspired</u> against him to kill him.
Definition: secretly plan an unlawful act
Synonyms:plotted, cogitated, connived, contrived, devised, intrigued, machinated, schemed
noun: conspiracy, conspirator
adjective: conspiratorial
verb: conspire
adverb: conspiratorially
Brutus and other Romans **conspired** to overthrow Caesar.
  38:9
But Onan knew that the heir would not be his; and it came to pass, when he went in to his brother's wife that he <u>emitted</u> on the ground, lest he should give an heir to his brother.
Definition: give of or out
Synonyms: discharged, flowed, gave off / given off, poured, voided
noun: emission, emitter
verb: emit
Uranium is an element that **emits** harmful radiation.
  39:10
And so it was, as she spoke to Joseph day by day, that he did not <u>heed</u> her, to lie with her or to be with her.
Definition: pay attention
Synonyms: listen, attend, hark, harke, hear, notice, cognizance
noun: heedfulness, heedlessness
adjective: heedful, heedless
verb: heed
adverb: heedfully
Prudent students listen when told to **heed** the words of the teacher.
  41:3
Then behold, seven other cows came up after them out of the river, ugly and <u>gaunt</u>, and stood by the other cows on the bank of the river.

Definition: thin or emasculated
Synonyms: lean, angular, bony, lank, lanky, meager, scrawny, skinny, spare, cadaverous, skeletal wasted
noun: gauntness
adjective: gaunt
adverb: gauntly
The survivors of Nazi concentration camps were **gaunt** from starvation and disease.
    41:23
Then behold, seven heads, withered, thin, and blighted by the east wind, sprang up after them.
Definition: plant disorder marked by withering or an organism causing it, harmful influence
Synonyms: blamed
noun: blight
verb: blight
Potato **blight** once so devastated the nation of Ireland that many were forced to emigrate or face starvation.
    41:30
"but after them seven years of famine will arise, and all the plenty will be forgotten in the land of Egypt; and the famine will deplete the land.
Definition: use up resources of
Synonyms: bankrupt, use up, drain, draw, draw down, exhaust, impoverish
noun: depletion
adjective: depletive
verb: deplete
Environmental conservationists fight to end the **depletion** of natural resources.
    41:42
Then Pharaoh took his signet ring off his hand and put it on Joseph's hand; and he clothed him in garments of fine linen and put a gold chain around his neck.
Definition: small seal
noun: signet
Official documents were not valid without the king's **signet** .
    41:51
Joseph called the name of the first born Manasseh. "For God has caused me to be forget all my toil and all my fathers house.
Definition: work hard and long
Synonyms: drudge, drudgery, grind, labor, moil, plugging, slavery, slog

ging, sweat, travail
noun: toiler, toothsomeness
adjective: toilsome
verb: toil
adverb: toilsomely
Farming families **toil** from sunrise to sunset to eke out a living on the land.
   42:4
But Jacob did not send Joseph's brother Benjamin with his brothers, for he said, Lest some calamity befall him."
Definition: happen to
Synonyms: betide, break, chance, come off, come to pass, develop, do, fall out, give, go, hap, occur, pass, rise, transpire,
verb: befall
The lighthearted family was blissfully unaware of the fate that would soon **befall** it.
   42:20
"And bring your youngest brother to me; so your words will be verified, and you shall not die." And they did so.
Definition: establish the truth, accuracy or reality of
Synonyms: confirmed, authenticated, bore out / borne out, corroborated, justified, substantiated, validated
noun: verifiability, verification, verifier
adjective: verifiable
verb: verify
Verification of visas often forces travellers to wait for hours at airports.
   42:27
But as one of them opened his sack to give his donkey feed at the encampment, he saw his monkey; and there it was, in the mouth of his sack.
Definition: make camp
Synonyms: campground
noun: encampment
verb: encamp
The general had his soldiers **encamp** in a swamp to avoid enemy forces.
   43:9
I myself will be surety for him; from my hand you shall require him. If I do not bring him back to you and set him before you, then let me bear the blame forever.
Definition: guarantee; one who gives a guarantee for another person
Synonyms: certainty, assurance
noun: surety, suretyship
The distraught mother was forced to use her house as bail **surety** that her

son would be present at his court date.

43:16

When Joseph saw Benjamin with them, he said to the <u>steward</u> of his house, "Take these men to my home, and slaughter an animal and make ready; for these men will dine with me at noon."

Definition: person in charge of household affairs
Synonyms: manager, officer, supervisor, administrator
noun: steward, stewardess, stewardship
verb: steward

Per the request of the host, the house **steward** fetched wine from the cellar.

43:28

And they answered, "Your servant our father is in good health; he is still alive." And they bowed their heads down and <u>prostrated</u> themselves.

Definition: lay flat
Synonyms: prone, supine
noun: prostration
adjective: prostrate
verb: prostrate

Moslems **prostrate** themselves when praying.

43:32

So they set him a place by themselves, and the Egyptians who ate with him by themselves; because the Egyptians could not eat food with the Hebrews, for that is an <u>abomination</u> to the Egyptians.

Definition: something hateful, disgusting
Synonyms: vile, loathsome, unpleasant
noun: abomination
verb: abominate

Idolatry is considered an **abomination** in numerous religious faiths.

44:5

'Is not this the one from which my lord drinks, and with which he indeed practices <u>divination</u>? You have done evil in so doing."

Definition: practice of foretelling the future
Synonyms: augury, prophecy
noun: divination

Some believe that fortune tellers are actually capable of **divining** the future.

45:3

Then Joseph said to his brothers, "I am Joseph; does my father still live?" But his brothers could not answer him for they were <u>dismayed</u> in his presence.

Definition: discouraged
Synonyms: appalled, consternated, daunted, horrified
noun: dismay

verb: dismay
Lack of academic success **dismayed** the student.
   45:9
Hasten and go up to my father and say to him, "Thus says your son Joseph: God has made me LORD of all Egypt: come down to me, do not <u>tarry.</u>
Definition: be slow in leaving
Synonyms: delay, dally, dawdle, linger, loiter, mull, poke, procrastinate, put off, trail
verb: tarry
After the final bell rings, most students do not **tarry** at school.
   47:9
And Jacob said to Pharaoh, "The days of the years of my <u>pilgrimage</u> are one hundred and thirty years; few and evil are the days of the years of my life, and they have been the days of the years of my life, and they have not attained to the days of the years of my life of my fathers in the days of the years of the life of my fathers in the days of their pilgrimage."
Definition: journey made by a pilgrim
noun: pilgrimage
Moslems are supposed to make a **pilgrimage** to the city of Mecca at least once in their lifetimes.
   47:13
Now there was no bread in all the land; for the famine was very severe, so that the land of Egypt and all the land of Canaan <u>languish</u> because of the famine.
Definition: become languid or discouraged
Synonyms: fail, decline, deteriorate, fade, flag, weaken
verb: languish
Numerous political dissidents **languish** in the prisons of China.
   47:22
Only the land of the priests he did not buy; for the priests had <u>rations allotted</u> to them by Pharaoh, and they ate their rations which Pharaoh gave them; therefore they did not sell their lands.
Definition: distribute as a share
Synonyms: share, allowance, bite, cut, lot, part, portion, quota, slice
noun: allotment
verb: allot
Food and shelter for refugees are **allotted** on the basis of need.
Definition: share or allotment (as of food)
Synonyms: allotments, allowances, apportionments, measures, parts, portions, quanta, quotes, shares, parcels, prorates
noun: ration

verb: ration
Military **rations** leave much to be desired to the tastebuds.
    49:10
The scepter shall not depart from Judah, Nor a lawgiver from between his feet, Until Shiloh comes; And to him shall be the obedience of the people,
Definition: staff signifying authority
noun: scepter
verb: scepter
The monarch's **scepter** was encrusted with various precious gems.
    49:13
"Zebulun shall dwell by the haven of the sea; he shall become a haven for ships, and his border shall adjoin Sidon.
Definition: be next to
Synonyms: abut, border, verge, touch
verb: adjoin
Washington, D.C. **adjoins** both Maryland and Virginia.
    49:17
Dan shall be a serpent by the way, A viper by the path, That bites the horses heels, So that its rider shall fall backward.
Definition: venomous snake
noun: viper
Scientists collect the venom of **vipers**.
    50:2
And Joseph commanded his servants the physicians to embalm his father. So the physicians embalmed Israel.
Definition: preserve (a corpse)
noun: embalmer, embalmment
verb: embalm
Corpses are **embalmed** so that they may be presented as undeteriorated as possible during the wake.

Random Review - Genesis

Match the numbered words with their lettered definitions. Check your answers in the back of the book.

1.	firmament		a.	forked-root herbs
2.	ewe		b.	harmful influence
3.	lentils		c.	sky
4.	mandrakes		d.	lay flat
5.	timbrel		e.	disaster
6.	blight		f.	something hateful
7.	calamity		g.	pea seeds
8.	prostrate		h.	ancient tambourine
9.	embalm		i.	preserve
10.	abomination		j.	sheep

Try These

Use the complete vocabulary list from the specified book to fill in the missing word for each verse.

Genesis

3:15
And I will put _____ Between you and the woman, And between your seed and her Seed; He shall bruise your heard, And you shall bruise his heel.

9:11
Thus I establish my _____ with you : Never again shall all flesh be cut off by the waters of the flood; never again shall there be a flood to destroy the earth.

15:16
But in the fourth generation they shall return here, for the _____ of Amorites is not yet complete.

EXODUS

EXODUS
1:13
So the Egyptians made the children of Israel serve with <u>rigor.</u>
Definition: severity
Synonyms: difficulty asperity, hardness, hardship, vicissitude
noun: rigor, rigorousness
adjective: rigorous
adverb: rigorously
Final exams are always **rigorous**.
2:3
But when she could no longer hide him, she took an ark of bulrushes for him, <u>daubed</u> it with asphalt and pitch, put the child in it, and laid it in the reeds by the river's bank.
Definition: smear
Synonyms: bedaubed, besmeared, dabbed, plastered, smudged
noun: daub
verb: daub
The doctor advised **daubing** ointment on the rash.
3:22
But every woman shall ask of her neighbor, namely, of her who dwells near her house, articles of silver, articles of gold, and clothing; and you shall put them on your sons and on your daughters. So shall <u>plunder</u> the Egyptians.
Definition: rob or take by force
Synonyms: knock over, loot, ransack, relieve
noun: plunder
verb: plunder
Pirates **plundered** ships on the high seas.
4:10
Then Moses said to the LORD, "Oh my LORD, I am not <u>eloquent</u>, neither before nor since You have spoken to Your servant, but I am slow of speech and slow of tongue.
Definition: forceful or persuasive in speech
Synonyms: articulate, fluent vocal, expressive, sententious
noun: eloquence
adjective: eloquent
verb: eloquently
Martin Luther King, Jr. was an **eloquent** public speaker.
5:3
So they said, "The God of the Hebrews has met with us. Please, let us go three days journey into the desert and sacrifice to the LORD our God, lest He fall upon us with <u>pestilence</u> or with the sword.

Definition: virulent or fatal contagious disease
Synonyms: epidemic, plague
noun: pestilence
adjective: pestilent, pestilential
adverb: pestilentially, pestilently
Antibiotics can prevent most forms of **pestilence**.
    5:21
And they said to them, "Let the LORD look on you and judge, because you have made us <u>abhorrent</u> in the sight of Pharaoh and in the sight of his servants, to put a sword in their hand to kill us."
Definition: hate
Synonyms: hateful, abominable, foul, horrid, odious, repugnant, invidious, obnoxious, repellent, repulsive
noun: abhorrence
adjective: abhorrent
verb: abhor
adverb: abhorrently
Many commuters find traffic jams **abhorrent**.
    7:18
And the fish that are in the river shall die, the river shall stink, and the Egyptians will <u>loathe</u> to drink the water of the river.
Definition: very reluctant
Synonyms: disinclined, afraid, averse, backward, hesitant, indisposed, shy, unwilling
adjective: loath
People generally **loathe** getting up early on Saturdays.
    9:31
Now the <u>flax</u> and the barley were stuck, for the barley was in the head and the flax was in bud.
Definition: plant from which linen is made
noun: flax
Flax can grow in several environments.
    9:32
But the wheat and the <u>spelt</u> we not struck, for they are late crops.
Definition: hard-grained kind of wheat
noun: spelt
Spelt is used in multi-grain bread.
    12:7
And they shall take some of the blood and put it on the two doorposts and on the <u>lintel</u> of the houses where they eat it.
Definition: horizontal piece over a door or window

noun: lintel
The **lintel** of a house can be decorated for holidays.
    12:14
So this day shall be to you a memorial; and you shall keep it as a feast to the LORD throughout your generations. You shall keep it as a feast by an everlasting <u>ordinance.</u>
Definition: municipal law
Synonyms: assize, canon, decree, edict, prescript, precept, prescription, regulation, rule, statute
noun: ordinance
Double parking violates city **ordinance.**
    12:16
On the first day there shall be a holy <u>convocation</u>, and on the seventh day there shall be a holy convocation for you. No manner of work shall be done on them; but that which everyone must eat that only may be prepared by you.
Definition: call together a meeting
Synonyms: assembly
noun: convocation
adjective: convocational
verb: convoke
The church membership holds a **convocation** every Tuesday afternoon.
    15:8
And with the blast of Your nostrils The waters were gathered together: The floods stood upright like a heap; And the depths <u>congealed</u> in the heart of the sea.
Definition: freeze, become thick or solid
Synonyms: hardened, caked, concreted, dried, indurated, set, solidified, coagulated, clotted, gelled, gelatinized, jelled, jellied
noun: congealment
verb: congeal
Melting cheese **congeals** rapidly at room temperature.
    16:31
And the house of Israel called its name Manna. And it was like white <u>coriander</u> seed, and the taste of it was like wafers made with honey.
Definition: European plant of the carrot family, or its seedlike fruit
noun: coriander
Corianders grow mainly in Europe.
    18:21
"Moreover you shall select from all the people able men, such as fear God, men of truth, hating <u>covetousness</u>; and place such over them to be rulers of

thousands, rulers of hundreds, rulers of fifties, and rulers of tens.
Definition: desire enviously
Synonyms: acquisitiveness, desirousness, graspingness, greediness
noun: coveter, covetousness
adjective: covetous
verb: covet
adverb: covetously
People often **covet** the possessions of others.
    21:14
"But if a man acts with <u>premeditation</u> against his neighbor, to kill him with guile, you shall take him from My alter, that he may die.
Definition: plan beforehand
Synonyms: plan, scheme
noun: premeditation
verb: premeditate
adverb: premeditatedly
Premeditated crimes carry harsher sentences than spontaneous ones.
    22:16
"And if a man entices a virgin who is not <u>betrothed</u>, and lies with her, he shall surely pay the bride-price for her to be his wife.
Definition: promise to marry
Synonyms: affianced, intended, engaged, contracted, plighted
noun: betrothal, betrothed
verb: betroth
To end the war between families, the woman was **betrothed** to one of her enemies.
    22:28
"You shall not <u>revile</u> God, nor curse a ruler of your people.
Definition: abuse
Synonyms: scold, baste, berate, dress down, jaw, lash, rag, rail, rant, vituperate
noun: revilement, reviler
verb: revile
Not long ago, people infected with HIV were **reviled**.
    23:11
"but the seventh year you shall let it rest and lie <u>fallow</u>, that the poor of your people may eat; and what they leave, the beasts of the field may eat. In like manner you shall do with your vineyard and your olive grove.
Definition: land plowed but not planted
Synonyms: uncultivated, inactive
noun: fallow, fallowness

adjective: fallow
verb: fallow
Fallow land is an inefficient use of farmland.
    23:13
"And in all that I have said to you, be <u>circumspect</u> and make no mention of the name of other gods,
nor let it be heard from your mouth.
Definition: careful,
Synonyms: cautious, calculating, careful, chary, consolidate, discreet, gingerly, considerate
noun: circumspection
adjective: circumspect
adverb: circumspectly
The detective **circumspectly** questioned the high ranking official.
    26:4
"And you shall make loops of blue yarn on the edge of the curtain on the <u>selvedge</u> of one set, and likewise you shall do on the outer edge of other curtain of the second set.
Definition: edge of woven fabric so formed as to prevent raveling
noun: selvedge
adjective: selvedged
Tailors are capable of **selvedging** many types of fabric.
    28:38
"So it shall be on Aaron's forehead, that Aaron may bear the iniquity of the holy things which the children of Israel <u>hallow</u> in all their holy gifts; and it shall always be on his forehead, that they may be accepted before the LORD.
Definition:consecrate
Synonyms: bless, devote, dedicate, sanctify
adjective: hallowed
verb: hallow
Holy places are often referred to as being "**hallowed** halls."
    29:13
"And you shall take all the fat that covers the <u>entrails</u>, the fatty lobe attached to the liver, and the two kidneys and the fat that is on them, and burn them on the alter.
Definition: intestines
Synonyms: guts, innards, insides, inwards, stuffing
noun: entrails
The **entrails** of animals are removed in slaughterhouses.
    29:33
"They shall eat those things with which the <u>atonement</u> was made, to

consecrate and to sanctify them; but a stranger shall not eat them, because they are holy.
Definition: make amends
Synonyms: conjunction, expiation
noun: atonement
verb: atone
Catholics **atone** in confession.
    30:18
"You shall make a <u>laver</u> of bronze, with its base also of bronze, for washing. You shall put it between the tabernacle of meeting and the alter. And you shall put water in it.
Definition: large basin to wash in
noun: laver
The golden **laver** is considered an artifact of great value.
    33:7
Moses took his tent and pitched it outside the camp, far from the camp, and called it the <u>tabernacle</u> of meeting. And it came to pass that everyone who sought the LORD went out to the tabernacle of meeting which was outside of the camp.
Definition: portable sanctuary, temple
Synonyms: church, shrine
noun: tabernacle
verb: tabernacling
The **tabernacle** was destroyed for housing "false gods."
    39:24
They made on the hem of the robe <u>pomegranates</u> of blue and purple and scarlet and fine linen thread.
Definition: tropical fruit with many seeds
noun: pomegranates
Pomegranates are a dietary staple in some cultures.
    40:3
"You shall put in the ark of the Testimony, and <u>partition</u> off the ark with the veil
Definition: something that divides
Synonyms: separation, detachment, dissolution, disunion, division, divorcement, rupture
noun: partition
verb: partition
The former nation of Yugoslavia has been **partitioned** into separate areas for Macedonians, Serbs, Croats, and Muslims.

Random Review - Exodus

Match the numbered words with their lettered definitions. Check your answers in the back of the book.

1. pestilence
2. flax
3. restitution
4. selvedge
5. entrails
6. coriander
7. betrothed
8. lintel
9. abhorrent
10. congealed

a. repayment
b. horizontal doorpiece
c. intestines
d. becomes solid
e. contagious disease
f. hateful
g. fabric edge
h. linen plant
i. promised to marry
j. carrot-like European plan

Try These

Use the complete vocabulary list from the specified book to fill in the missing word for each verse.

Exodus

7:18
And the fish that are in the river shall die, the river shall stink, and the EgyptianS will _____ to drink the water of the river.

15:8
And with the blast of Your nostrils The waters were gathered together: The floods stood upright like a heap; And the depths _____ in the heart of the sea.

29:33
"They shall eat those things with which the _____ was made, to consecrate and to sanctify them; but a stranger shall not eat them, because they are holy.

LEVITICUS

LEVITICUS
5:18
"And he shall bring to priest a ram without blemish from the flock, with your valuation, as a trespass offering. So the priest shall make atonement for him regarding his ignorance in which he <u>erred</u> and did not know it, and it shall be forgiven.
Definition: be or do wrong
Synonyms: deviated, strayed, wandered
verb: err
"To **err** is human, but forgiveness is divine."
6:2
"If a person sins and commits a trespass against the LORD by lying to his neighbor about what was delivered to him for safekeeping, or about a pledge, or about a robbery, or if he has <u>extorted</u> from his neighbor.
Definition: obtain by force or improper pressure
Synonyms: exacted, gouged, pinched, screwed, shook down / shaken down, wrenched, squeezed
noun: extorter, extortion, extortioner, extortionist
adjective: extortive
verb: extort
The Vietnamese gangs attempted to **extort** money from recent immigrants.
8:13
then Moses brought Aaron's sons and put tunics on them, <u>girded</u> them with sashes, and put hats on them, as the LORD had commanded Moses.
Definition: encircle or fasten as with a belt
Synonyms: belted, banded, girdled
verb: gird
As the final component of their uniforms, the soldiers **girded** themselves with ammunition clips.
11:3
'Among the beasts, whatever divides the hoof, having cloven hooves and chewing the <u>cud</u>-that you may eat.
Definition: food chewed by ruminating animals
noun: cud
Cows chew regurgitated food called **cud**.
11:4
'Nevertheless these you shall not eat among those that chew the cud or those that have cloven: the camel, because it chews the cud but does not have <u>cloven</u> hooves, is unclean to you;
Definition: hoof divided by a cleft
noun: cleft

adjective: cloven
Horses have **cloven** hooves.
    11:36

'Nevertheless a spring or a <u>cistern</u>, in which there is plenty of water, shall be clean, but whatever touches any such carcass becomes unclean.
Definition: underground water tank
noun: cistern
Small villages may receive their water supply from a **cistern**.
    17:4

"and does not bring it to the door of the tabernacle of meeting, to offer an offering to the LORD before the tabernacle of the LORD, bloodguilt shall be <u>imputed</u> to that man. He has shed blood; and that man shall be cut off from among his people,
Definition: credit or blame on a person or cause
Synonyms: ascribed, accredited, assigned, charged
noun: imputability, imputation
adjective: imputable, imputative
verb: verb
adverb: imputatively
Voters **impute** their politicians for the economic and social problems of America.
    19:9

'When you reap the harvest of your land, you shall not wholly reap the corners of your field, nor shall you gather the <u>gleanings</u> of your harvest.
Definition: things acquired little by little
Synonyms: culling, extracting, garnering, gathering
noun: gleaner
adjective: gleanable
verb: glean
Knowledge may be **gleaned** by listening to the conversations of others.
    19:20

Whoever lies carnally with a woman who is betrothed as a concubine to another man, and who has not all been redeemed nor given her freedom, for this there shall be <u>scourging</u>; but they shall not be put to death because she was not free.
Definition: lash or punish severely
Synonyms: whipping, flagellating, striping, thrashing, whaling
noun: scourge, scourger
verb: scourge
The general's family was **scourged** for his failure in battle.
    23:14

You shall eat neither bread nor parched grain for fresh grain until the same day that you have brought an offering to your God; it shall be a statute forever throughout your generations in all your dwellings.
Definition: toast or shrivel with dry heat
Synonyms: dried, dehydrated, desiccated, seared
verb: parch
Physical exertion during the summer months leaves one **parched.**
  24:11
And the Israelite woman's son blasphemed the name of the LORD and cursed; and so they brought him to Moses. (His mother's name was Shelomith the daughter of Dibri, of the tribe of Dan.)
Definition: speak irreverence toward God or anything sacred
Synonyms: cursing, execration, imprecation, profanity, swearing
noun: blasphemer
verb: blaspheme
Many icons of contemporary culture are considered **blasphemous** by religious groups.

Random Review - Leviticus

Match the numbered words with their lettered definitions. Check your answers in the back of the book.

1. extorted
2. cud
3. scourging
4. blasphemed
5. girded
6. cistern
7. imputed
8. cloven
9. parched
10. gleanings

a. spoke irreverently of God
b. underground water tank
c. fastened
d. blamed
e. improperly pressured
f. shriveled by heat
g. punishing severely
h. divided hoof
i. acquired little by little
j. chewed by animals

Try These

Use the complete vocabulary list from the specified book to fill in the missing word for each verse.

Leviticus

6:2
"If a person sins and commits a trespass against the Lord by lying to his neighbor about what was delivered to him for safekeeping, or about a pledge, or about a robbery, or if he has _____ from his neighbor.

11:4
'Nevertheless these you shall not eat among those that chew the cud or those that have cloven: the camel, because it chews the cud but does not have _____ hooves, is unclean to you;

24:11
And the Israelite woman's son _____ the name of the LORD and cursed; and so they brought him to Moses. (His mother's name was Shelomith the daughter of Dibri, of the tribe of Dan.)

NUMBERS

NUMBERS
5:7
Then he shall confess the sin which he has done. He shall make <u>restitution</u> for his trespass in full value plus one-fifth of it, and give it to the one he has wronged.
Definition: act of restoring something or paying someone
Synonyms: amends, indemnity, recompose, compensation
noun: restitution
Asbestos manufacturers were ordered to pay **restitution** to the victims.
11:29
Then Moses said to him, "Are you <u>zealous</u> for my sake? Oh, that all the LORD's people were prophets and that the LORD would put His Spirit upon them?"
Definition: filled with enthusiasm
Synonyms: passion, ardor, fervor, fire, hurrah
noun: zealousness
adjective: zealous
adverb: zealously
Some environmentalists, such as Greenpeace, are **zealous** about their cause.
14:18
The LORD is longsuffering and abundant in mercy, forgiving iniquity and <u>transgression</u>; but He by no means clears the guilty, visiting the iniquity of the fathers on the children to the third and fourth generation.
Definition: sin
Synonyms: infringement, trespass, violation, infraction, contravention, breach
noun: transgression, transgressor
adjective: transgressive
Sinners **transgress** against the LORD.
15:30
But the person who does anything <u>presumptuously</u>, whether he is native born or a stranger, that one brings reproach on the LORD, and he shall be cut off from among his people.
Definition: too bold or forward
Synonyms: brashly, confidently, overconfidently, presumingly, forwardly, gaily
adjective: presumptuously
adverb: presumptuously
The **presumptuous** child demanded $700 to purchase a bicycle.
16:2
and they rose up before Moses with some of the children of Israel, two

hundred and fifty leaders of the congregation, representatives of the congregation, men of <u>renown.</u>
Definition: state of being widely known and honored
Synonyms: fame, notoriety, reputation
noun: renown
adjective: renowned
The ambassador gained great **renown** for negotiating the peace treaty.
    22:30
So the donkey said to Balaam, "Am I not your donkey on which you have ridden, ever since I became yours, to this day? Was I ever <u>disposed</u> to do this to you?"
Definition: tendency towards
Synonyms: willing, fain, inclined, prone, ready, biased, ordered
noun: disposal, disposer
adjective: disposable
verb: dispose
New York's governor was **disposed** to granting a pardon to the convict.
    23:7
An he took up his oracle and said; "Balak the king of Moab has brought me from Aram, From the mountains of the east. "Come, curse Jacob for me. And come, <u>denounce</u> Israel!
Definition: criticize severely, inform against
Synonyms: blame, censure, condemn, reprobate, reprehend, cutup
noun: denouncement, denouncer
verb: denounce
Terrorists must be publicly **denounced.**
    24:17
"I see Him, but not now; I behold Him but not near; A Star shall come out of Jacob; A Scepter shall rise out of Israel, And batter the brow of Moab, And destroy all sons of <u>tumult.</u>
Definition: violent agitation of mind or feelings
Synonyms: commotions, agitations, confusions, turbulences, disorderly
noun: tumult, tumultuousness
adjective: tumultuously
verb: tumultuously
The attempted coup left the country in a very **tumultuous** situation.
    25:7
Now when the Phinehas the son of Eleazar, the son of Aaron the priest, saw it he rose from among the congregation and took a <u>javelin</u> in his hand;
Definition: light spear

noun: javelin
Javelins were once used as weapons of war but now are thrown as an Olympic sport.

31:28
"And <u>levy</u> a tribute for the LORD on the men of war who went out to battle: one of every five hundred of the persons, the cattle, the donkeys, and the sheep;

Definition: imposition or collection of a tax
Synonyms: tax, assessment, duty, impost, tariff, exact, impose, put upon
noun: levy, levier
adjective: leviable
verb: levy
To increase the coffers new **levies** were imposed on imported petroleum products.

Random Review - Numbers

Match the numbered words with their lettered definitions. Check your answers in the back of the book.

1. zealous
2. transgression
3. renown
4. tumult
5. javelin
6. levy
7. denounce
8. restitution
9. disposed
10. presumptuously

a. light spear
b. tax collection
c. sin
d. too forward
e. criticize
f. enthusiastic
g. tendency toward
h. violent agitation
i. payback
j. widely known

Try These

Use the complete vocabulary list from the specified book to fill in the missing word for each verse.

Numbers

14:18
The Lord is longsuffering and abundant in mercy, forgiving iniquity and _____ ; but He by no means clears the guilty, visiting the iniquity of the fathers on the children to the third and fourth generation.

22:30
So the donkey said to Balaam, "Am I not your donkey on which you have ridden, ever since I became yours, to this day? Was I ever _____ _____ to do this to you?"

DEUTERONOMY

DEUTERONOMY
> 2:1

"Then we turned and journeyed into the wilderness of the Way of the Red Sea, as the LORD spoke to me, and we <u>skirted</u> Mount Seir for many days.

Definition: pass around the edges of
Synonyms: bypassed, circumnavigated, circumvented, sidestepped
noun: skirt
verb: skirt

It is better to **skirt** trouble rather than chase after it.

> 2:7

"For the LORD your God has blessed you in all the work of your hand. He knows your <u>trudging</u> through this great wilderness. These forty years the LORD your God has been with you; you have lacked nothing.

Definition: walk, or march steadily, and with difficulty
Synonyms: plodding, slogging, slopping, toiling
verb: trudge

During their attempted attack on Moscow, German troops **trudged** through mud and snow.

> 2:30

"But Sihon king of Heshbon would not let us pass through, for the LORD your God hardened his spirit and made his hear <u>obstinate</u>, that He might deliver him into your hand, as it is this day.

Definition: unwilling to submit to control
Synonyms: stubborn
noun: obstinacy, obstinateness
adjective: obstinate
adverb: obstinately

Obstinate managers often miss new opportunities when economic conditions change.

> 2:36

"From Aroer, which is on the bank of the River Arnon, and from the city that is in the <u>ravine</u>, as far as Gilead, there not one city too strong for us; the LORD our God delivered all to us.

Definition: narrow steep-sided valley
Synonyms: arroyo, chasm, cleft, clove, gap, gorge, gulch
noun: ravine

Fleeing refugees were able to hide from advancing troops in a hidden **ravine**.

> 8:9

"a land of wheat in which you will eat bread without <u>scarcity</u>, in which you will lack nothing, a land whose stones are iron and out of whose hills you can dig copper.

Definition: not plentiful, rare
Synonyms: poverty, scarceness, insufficience, paucity
noun: scarcity, scarceness
adjective: scarce
adverb: scarcely
The concept of **scarcity** is a principle component of the science of economics.

15:17

"then you shall take an <u>awl</u> and thrust it through his ear to the door, and he shall be your servant forever. Also to your maidservant you shall do likewise.
Definition: hole-making tool
noun: awl
Awls are used to pierce ears.

16:9

"You shall count seven weeks for yourself; begin to count the seven weeks from the time you begin to put the <u>sickle</u> to the grain.
Definition: curved short-handled blade
noun: sickle
Many idealized manifestations of death often carry a **sickle**.

20:19

"When you <u>besiege</u> a city for a long time, while making war against it to take it, you shall not destroy its trees by wielding an ax against them; if you can eat of them, do not cut them down to use in the siege, for the tree of the field is man's food.
Definition: lay siege to
Synonyms: beleaguer, beset, blockade, invest
noun: besieger
verb: besiege
The ancient city of Troy was **besieged** by the Greeks.

21:20

"And they shall say to the elders of his city, 'This son of ours is stubborn and rebellious; he will not obey our voice; he is a <u>glutton</u> and a drunkard."
Definition: one who eats to excess
noun: glutton, gluttonousness, gluttony
adjective: gluttonous
adverb: gluttonously
Gluttony is acceptable on the Thanksgiving holiday.

22:8

"When you build a new house, then you shall make a <u>parapet</u> for your roof, that you may not bring bloodguiltiness on your house if anyone falls from it.
Definition: protecting rampart in a fort

Synonyms: bulwark, bastion, breastwork, rampart
noun: parapet
adjective: parapeted
Settlements once used **parapets** to guard against invasion.
    23:1
"He who is <u>emasculated</u> by crushing or mutilation shall not enter the congregation of the LORD.
Definition: castrate, weaken
Synonyms: unnerved, unmanned, unstrung
noun: emasculation, emasculator
verb: emasculate
Sadam Hussein is effectively **emasculated** by the presence of foreign troops in Iraq.

Random Review - Deuteronomy

Match the numbered words with their lettered definitions. Check your answers in the back of the book.

1. obstinate
2. ravine
3. scarcity
4. awl
5. sickle
6. besiege
7. glutton
8. parapet
9. emasculated
10. trudging

a. rare
b. curved, shorthandled blade
c. excessive eater
d. unwilling to submit
e. protecting rampart
f. walking with difficulty
g. hole-making tool
h. castrated
i. lay siege to
j. narrow valley

Try These

Use the complete vocabulary list from the specified book to fill in the missing word for each verse.

Deuteronomy

2:30
"But Sihon king of Heshbon would not let us pass through, for the Lord your God hardened his spirit and made his hear _____, that He might deliver him into your hand, as it is this day.

23:1
"He who is _____ by crushing or mutilation shall not enter the congregation of the Lord.

JOSHUA

JOSHUA
8:4
And he commanded them, saying: "Behold, you shall lie in <u>ambush</u> against the city, behind the city. Do not go very far from the city, but all of you be ready.
Definition: trap by which a surprise attack is made from a place of hiding
Synonyms: surprise, lay for, waylay
noun: ambush
adjective: ambush
Military strategists often devise ingenious **ambushes**.
8:10
Then Joshua rose up early in the morning and <u>mustered</u> the people, and went up, he and the elders of Israel, before the people to Ai.
Definition: assemble, rouse
Synonyms: signed on, rallied, gathered, enlisted, enrolled, joined up
noun: musters
verb: muster
A persuasive politician can **muster** his constituency.
20:9
These were the cities of Israel and for the stranger who <u>sojourned</u> among them, that whoever killed any person accidently might flee there, and not die by the end of the avenger of the blood until he stood before the congregation.
Definition: reside temporarily
Synonyms: visited, stayed, stopped over, tarried
noun: sojourn, sojourner
verb: sojourn
Muslims **sojourn** to Mecca and Medina to comply with their religious obligations.

JUDGES

JUDGES

    4:6

Then she sent and called for Barak the son of Abinoam from Kedesh in the Naphtali, and said to him, "Has not the LORD God of Israel commanded, saying, "Go and <u>deploy</u> troops at Mount Tabor; take with you ten thousand men of the sons of Naphtali and of the sons of Zebulun;

Definition: spread out for battle
noun: deployment
The general **deployed** his troops on several fronts along the border.

    5:10

"Speak, you who ride on white donkeys, Who sit in judge's <u>attire</u>,
And who walk along the road.

Definition: dress
Synonyms: clothing, apparel, clad, garment, raiment
noun: attire
verb: attire
Proper **attire** is required for an interview.

    5:17

Gilead stayed beyond the Jordan,
And why did Dan remain on ships?
Asher continued at the seashore,
And stayed by his <u>inlets</u>.

Definition: bay or recess in a shore
Synonyms: arms, bays, bayous, bights, coves, firths, gulfs, harbors, sloughs
noun: inlet
Inlets provide the best fishing.

    6:4

Then they would encamp against them and destroy the produce of the earth as far as Gaza, and leave no <u>sustenance</u> for Israel, neither sheep, nor ox, nor donkeys.

Definition: nourishment
Synonyms: food, aliment, nutriment, pabulum, pap
noun: sustenance
Many types of food should be used as **sustenance**.

    9:14

"Then all the trees said to the <u>bramble</u>,
'You come and reign over us!"

Definition: prickly shrub
noun: bramble
adjective: brambly
Brambles will cut your skin if you run through the woods.

11:37
Then she said to her father, "Let this thing be done for me: let me alone for two months, that I may go and wander on the mountains and <u>bewail</u> my virginity, my friends and I."
Definition: lament
Synonyms: deplore, bemoan, grieve, moan, weep
verb: bewail
The people **bewailed** the death of their greatest leader.

12:5
The Gileadites seized the <u>fords</u> of Jordan before the Ephraimites arrived. And when any Ephraimite who escaped said, "Let me cross over," the men of Gilead would say to him, "Are you an Ephraimite?" If he said, "No,"
Definition: place to wade across a stream
noun: ford
verb: ford
The cowboys **forded** the river at its shallowest point.

14:1
Now Samson went down to Timnah, and saw a woman in Timnah of the daughters of the <u>Philistines</u>.
Definition: one who is smugly indifferent to ideas or art
Synonyms: middlebrows
noun: philistine
adjective: philistine
Philistines don't appreciate the finer things in life.

16:16
And it came to pass, when she pestered him daily with her words and pressed him, so that his soul was <u>vexed</u> to death,
Definition: trouble, distress, or annoy
Synonyms: bothered, chafed, exercised, fretted, galled, irked, provoked, ruffled
noun: vexation, vexatiousness
adjective: vexatious
verb: vex
adverb: vexatiously
She was **vexed** by her inability to remember theorems of geometry.

16:19
Then she <u>lulled</u> him to sleep on her knees, and called for a man and had him shave off the seven locks of his head. Then she began to torment him, and his strength left.
Definition: make or become quiet or relaxed
Synonyms: calmed, allayed, soothed, settled, becalmed

noun: lull
verb: lull
The soldiers were **lulled** into making careless mistakes, then the tables were turned on them.
    16:21
Then the Philistines took him and put out his eyes, and brought him down to Gaza. They bound him with bronze fetters, and he became a grinder in prison.
Definition: chain or shackle for the feet
Synonyms: shackles, bonds, chains, gyves, irons
noun: fetter
verb: fetter
The prisoners were **fettered** into place.
    19:19
"although we have both straw and fodder for our donkeys, and bread and wine for myself, for your maidservant, and for the young man who is your servant; there is no lack of anything."
Definition: food for livestock
noun: fodder
verb: fodder
We have sufficient **fodder** in the barn to survive a harsh winter.
    20:5
"And the men of Gibeah rose against me, and surrounded the house at night because of me. They intended to kill me, but instead they ravished my concubine so that she died.
Definition: seize and take away by violence, rape
Synonyms: defiled, forced, violated
noun: ravisher, ravishment
verb: ravish
The robbers **ravished** the church congregation of its collections.
    20:6
"So they took hold of my concubine, cut her in pieces, and sent her throughout all the territory of inheritance of Israel, because they committed lewdness and outrage in Israel.
Definition: sexually unchaste; salacious
Synonyms: licentiousness, fastness, lecherousness, lustfulness
noun: lewdness
adjective: lewd
adverb: lewdly
Many examples of **lewdness** are considered constitutionally protected free speech.

20:30
And the children of Israel went up against the children of Benjamin on the third day, and put themselves in battle <u>array</u> against Gibeah as at the other times.
Definition: arrange in order; imposing group
Synonyms: order, arrange, dispose, organize
noun: array
verb: array
The collector displayed an impressive **array** of weaponry.

Random Review - Joshua & Judges

Match the numbered words with their lettered definitions. Check your answers in the back of the book.

1.	ambush	a.	assembled
2.	mustered	b.	lament
3.	deploy	c.	smugly indifferent to ideas and art
4.	bramble	d.	foot shackles
5.	bewail	e.	spread out for battle
6.	ford	f.	food for livestock
7.	Philistine	g.	sexually unchaste
8.	fetters	h.	prickly shrub
9.	fodder	i.	wade across a stream
10.	lewdness	j.	trap

Try These

Use the complete vocabulary list from the specified book to fill in the missing word for each verse.

Joshua

8:10
Then Joshua rose up early in the morning and _____ the people, and went up, he and the elders of Israel, before the people to Ai.

Judges

6:4
Then they would encamp against them and destroy the produce of the earth as far as Gaza, and leave no _____ for Israel, neither sheep, nor ox, nor donkeys.

16:21
Then the Philistines took him and put out his eyes, and brought him down to Gaza. They bound him with bronze _____, and he became a grinder in prison.

SAMUEL I

SAMUEL I
1:15
And Hannah answered and said, "No, my lord, I am a woman of sorrowful spirit. I have drunk neither wine nor <u>intoxicating</u> drink, but have poured out my soul before the LORD."
Definition: make drunk
Synonyms: rousing, stimulating, stirring
noun: intoxicant, intoxication
adjective: intoxicant
adverb: intoxicatedly
The demagogue was **intoxicated** with his own power.

1:22
But Hannah did not go up, for she said to her husband, "I will not go up until the child is <u>weaned</u>; then I will take him, that he may appear before the LORD and remain there forever."
Definition: free from dependence
verb: wean
Before being released into the wild, zoo animals must be **weaned** from human dependence.

2:14
Then he would thrust it into the pan, or kettle, or <u>cauldron</u>, or pot; and the priest would take for himself all that the fleshhook brought up. So they did in Shiloh to all Israelites who came there.
Definition: large kettle
noun: cauldron
The witch combined her spell components in a large **cauldron**.

3:13
"For I have told him that I will judge his house forever for the iniquity that he knows, because his sons made themselves <u>vile</u>, and he did not restrain them.
Definition: thoroughly bad or contemptible
Synonyms: base, despicable, ignoble, low, sordid, squalid, wretched, offensive, atrocious, loathsome
noun: vileness
adjective: vile
adverb: vilely
The murder was so **vile** that the prosecutor asked for the death penalty.

4:7
So the Philistines were afraid, for they said, "God has come into the camp!" And they said, '<u>Woe</u> to us! For such a thing has never happened before."
Definition: deep suffering

Synonyms: sorrow, affliction, anguish, grief, heartbreak
noun: woe
Prophets often predicted the **woes** of the world.
    5:4
And when they arose early the next morning, there was Dagon, fallen on his face to the ground before the ark of the LORD. The head of Dagon and both palms of its hands were broken off on the <u>threshold</u>; only the torso of Dagon was left of it.
Definition: sill of a door, beginning stage
Synonyms: verge, brink, edge, point
noun: threshold
Boot camps increase the **threshold** of pain for potential soldiers.
    7:9
And Samuel took a <u>suckling</u> lamb and offered it as a whole burnt offering to the LORD. Then Samuel cried out to the LORD for Israel, and the LORD answered him.
Definition: young, unweaned animal
Synonyms: nursing, breast-feeding, nourishing
noun: suckling
verb: suckle
Zoo keepers **suckle** the young animals in their care.
    8:14
"And he will take the best of your fields, your vineyards, and your olive <u>groves</u>, and give them to his servants.
Definition: small group of trees
noun: grove
The **grove** of the desert formed an oasis.
    10:19
"But you have today rejected your God, who Himself saved you out of your <u>adversities</u> and your tribulations; and you have said to Him, "No, but set a king over us!" Now therefore, present yourselves before the LORD by your tribes and by your clans."
Definition: hard times
Synonyms: misfortune, mischances, mishaps, tragedies
noun: adversity
adjective: adverse
Succeeding under **adverse** conditions is often required.
    10:26
And Saul also went home to Gibeah; and <u>valiant</u> men went with him, whose hearts God had touched.

Definition: brave or heroic
Synonyms: audacious, aweless, bold, courageous, dauntless, doughty, fearless, gallant
noun: valiant
adjective: valiant
verb: valiantly
Medieval knights were often called valiant.

13:3

And Jonathan attacked the garrison of the Philistines that was in Geba, and the Philistines heard of it. Then Saul blew the trumpet throughout all the land saying, "Let the Hebrews hear!"
Definition: military post or the troops stationed there
noun: garrison
verb: garrison
Spaniards left garrisons to defend their newly conquered territory in the New World.

13:12

"then I said, "The Philistines will now come down on me at Gilgal, and I have not made supplication to the LORD." Therefore I felt compelled, and offered a burnt offering."
Definition: cause through necessity
Synonyms: forced, coerced, constrained, obliged, shotgunned
noun: compeller
adjective: compellable
verb: compel
adverb: compellingly
Though the soldier did not want to fight in the war, he was compelled to by his superiors.

13:21

and the charge for a sharpening was a pim for the plowshares, the mattocks, the forks, and the axes, and to set the points of the goads.
Definition: plow part that cuts the earth
noun: plowshare
The farmer, tired of having to replace worn plowshares, is saving to purchase modern equipment.

14:47

So Saul established his sovereignty over Israel, and fought against all his enemies on every side, against Moab, against the people of Ammon, against Edom, against the kings of Zobah, and against the Philistines. Wherever he turned, he harassed them.
Definition: supreme rulership

Synonyms: supremacy, ascendency, ascendant, dominance, domination, dominion, preeminence, preponderance
noun: sovereign, sovereignty
adverb: sovereignly
Secondary economic boycotts violate the **sovereignty** of nations.

15:14
But Samuel said, "What then is this <u>bleating</u> of the sheep in my ears, and the blowing of the oxen which I hear?"
Definition: cry of a sheep or goat or a sound like it
Synonyms: griping, crabbing, fussing, squawking, yammering
noun: bleat
verb: bleat
Sheep herders may be soothed by the sound of **bleating**.

16:7
But the LORD said to Samuel, "Do not look at his appearance or at the height of his <u>stature</u>, because I have refused him. For the LORD does not see as man sees; for man looks at the outward appearance, but the LORD looks at the heart."
Definition: height; status gained by achievement
Synonyms: quality, caliber, merit, value, virtue, worth
noun: stature
Newly inaugurated presidents have great stature in the eyes of the people.

16:12
So he sent and brought him in. Now he was <u>ruddy</u>, with bright eyes, and good looking. And the LORD said, "Arise, anoint him; for this is the one!"
Definition: reddish
Synonyms: florid, flush, glowing, rubicund, sanguine
noun: ruddiness
adjective: ruddy
After finishing first in race, the runner was **ruddy** with joy.

17:28
Now Eliab his oldest brother heard when he spoke to the men; and Eliab's anger was aroused against David, and he said, "Why did you come down here? And with whom have you left those few sheep in the wilderness? I know your pride and the <u>insolence</u> of your heart, for you have come down to see the battle."
Definition: contemptuously rude
Synonyms: boldness, disrespect, impertinence, impudence
noun: insolence
adjective: insolent
adverb: insolently

A woman reprimanded her **insolent** child.
    17:42
And when the Philistine looked about and saw David, he <u>disdained</u> him; for he was but a youth, ruddy and good looking.
Definition: feeling of contempt
Synonyms: despised, abhorred, condemned, looked down, scorned, scouted
noun: disdain, disdainfulness
adjective: disdainfully
verb: disdain
adverb: disdainfully
Wealthy elitists glanced with **disdain** at the homeless people.
    17:51
Therefore David ran and stood over the Philistine, took his sword and drew it out of his <u>sheath</u> and killed him, and cut off his head with it. And when the Philistine saw that their champion was dead they fled.
Definition: covering (as for a blade)
Synonyms: skin, sheathing
noun: sheath
As a gesture of peace, the factions **sheathed** their weapons.
    18:8
Then Saul was very angry, and the saying displeased him; and he said "They have ascribed to David ten thousands, and to me they have <u>ascribed</u> but thousands. Now what more can he have but the kingdom?"
Definition: attribute
Synonyms: accredited, assigned, attributed, charged, credited, imputed
noun: ascription
adjective: ascribable
verb: ascribe
The Iliad is **ascribed** to the poet Homer.
    23:13
So David and his men, about six hundred, arose and departed from Keilah and went wherever they could go. Then it was told Saul that David had escaped from Keilah; so he halted the <u>expedition.</u>
Definition: long journey for work or research or the people making this
Synonyms: journey, peregrination, travel, travels, trek, trip
noun: expedition
Spaniards launched several **expeditions** to discover El Dorado, the fabled "city of gold."
    24:3
So he came to the sheepfolds by the road, where there was a cave; and Saul went in to attend to his needs. (David and his men were staying in the

recesses of the cave.)
Definition: indentation, in a line or surface
Synonyms: adjourns, dissolves, interior, rises, terminates
noun: recess
verb: recess
Though she professed to believe his alibi, in the **recesses** of her mind she thought him guilty.

24:12
Let the LORD judge between you and me, and let the LORD avenge me on you. But my hand shall not be against you.
Definition: take vengeance for
Synonyms: redress, revenge, vindicate
noun: avenger
verb: avenge
The remnants of the military vowed to **avenge** their defeat at the hands of their enemies.

26:24
"And indeed, as your life was valued much this day in my eyes, so let my life be valued much in the eyes of the LORD, and let Him deliver me out of all tribulation."
Definition: suffering from oppression
Synonyms: trial, tribulation, affliction, calvary, cross, crucible, ordeal, visitation
noun: tribulation
Despite great **tribulations**, their spirits were not broken.

28:14
So he said to her, What is his form?" And she said,"An old man is coming up, and he is covered with a mantle." And Saul perceived that it was Samuel, and he stooped with his face to the ground and bowed down.
Definition: sleeveless cloak
noun: mantle
verb: mantle
A colorful **mantle** sells for $45.00 in the marketplace.

SAMUEL II

SAMUEL II
  1:24
"O daughters of Israel, weep over Saul, Who clothed you in scarlet, with luxury; Who put ornaments of gold on your <u>apparel.</u>
Definition: clothing
Synonyms: clothe, array, attire, clad, dress, garb, garment, raiment, clothes
noun: apparel
The clothing outlet offers a wide range of **apparel**.
  5:11
Then Hiram king of Tyre sent messengers to David, and cedar trees, and carpenters and <u>masons</u>. And they built David a house.
Definition: workman who builds with stone or brick
noun: mason, masonry
verb: mason
Masons are trained at trade schools.
  16:7
Also Shimei said thus when he cursed; "Come out! Come out! You bloodthirsty man, you <u>rogue</u>!
Definition: dishonest or mischievous person
Synonyms: villain, blackguard, heel, knave, miscreant, rascal, reprobate, scoundrel, swindler, cheat, defrauder, flimflammer, gyp
noun: rogue, roguery, roguishness
adjective: roguish
verb: rogue
adverb: roguishly
Robin Hood was considered a **rogue** by the local authorities.
  20:3
Now David came to his house at Jerusalem. And the king took the ten women, his concubines whom he had left to keep the house, and put them in <u>seclusion</u> and supported them, but did not go in to them. So they were shut up to the day of their death living in widowhood.
Definition: shut off alone
Synonyms: reclusion, retirement, sequestration
noun: secludedness, seclusion, seclusiveness
adjective: secluded, seclusive
verb: seclude
adverb: secludedly
For their honeymoon, the couple chose a **secluded** island paradise.
  20:12
But Amasa <u>wallowed</u> in his blood in the middle of the highway. And when

the man saw that all the people stood still, he moved Amasa from the highway to the field and threw a garment over him, when he saw that everyone who came upon him halted.
Definition: roll about in deep mud; live with excessive pleasure
Synonyms: weltered, blundered, floundered, lurched, stumbled, basked, indulged
noun: wallow
verb: wallow
Rather than **wallow** in his own self-pity, the recently widowed man chose to move on with his life.

20:15
Then they came and besieged him in Abel of Beth Maachah; and they cast up a siege mound against the city, and it stood by the rampart. And all the people who were with Joab battered the wall to throw it down.
Definition: embankment of a fortification
Synonyms: bulwark, bastion, breastwork, parapet
noun: rampart
The fort's **ramparts** are badly in need of repair.

22:12
He made darkness canopies around Him, Dark waters and thick clouds of the skies.
Definition: overhanging cover
noun: canopy
verb: canopy
The landscaper crafted this beautiful flowered **canopies**.

Random Review - Samuel I & II

Match the numbered words with their lettered definitions. Check your answers in the back of the book.

1.	intoxicating	a.	military post
2.	cauldron	b.	indentations
3.	garrison	c.	journey
4.	plowshares	d.	clothing
5.	sovereignty	e.	supreme rulership
6.	insolence	f.	build with stone or brick
7.	expedition	g.	suffering from oppression
8.	recesses	h.	making drunk
9.	tribulation	i.	overhanging cover
10.	apparel	j.	overcame
11.	mason	k.	part that cuts earth
12.	rogue	l.	roll about
13.	canopies	m.	rudeness
14.	vanquished	n.	mischievous person
15.	wallowed	o.	large kettle

Try These

Use the complete vocabulary list from the specified book to fill in the missing word for each verse.

Samuel I

3:13
"For I have told him that I will judge his house forever for the iniquity that he knows, because his sons made themselves _____, and he did not restrain them.

Samuel II

20:12
But Amasa _____ in his blood in the middle of the highway. And when the man saw that all the people stood still, he moved Amasa from the highway to the field and threw a garment over him, when he saw that everyone who came upon him halted.

KINGS I

KINGS I
1:31
Then Bathsheba bowed with her face to the earth, and did <u>homage</u> to the king, and said, "Let my Lord King David live forever."
Definition: reverent regard
Synonyms: honor, deference, obeisance, reverence
noun: homage
We should pay **homage** to the sacrifices of their predecessors.
1:42
While he was still speaking, there came Jonathan, the son of Abiathar the priest. And Adonijah said to him, "Come in for you are a <u>prominent</u> man, and bring good tidings."
Definition: something that stands out
Synonyms: noticeable, conspicuous, famous, celebrated, distinguished, eminent, famed, illustrious, notable, prestigious
noun: prominence
adjective: prominent
adverb: prominently
Prominent business people effectively control the town government.
2:8
"And see, you have home with Shimei the son of Gera, a Benjamite from Bahurim, who cursed me with a <u>malicious</u> curse in the day when I went to Mahanaim. But he came down to meet me at the Jordan, and I swore to him by the LORD saying, "I will not put you to death with the sword."
Definition: ill will
Synonyms: catty, spiteful, evil, hateful, malevolent, malign, malignant, nasty, rancorous, spiteful, vicious, wicked
noun: malice, maliciousness
adjective: malicious
adverb: maliciously
The crime was committed with **malicious** intent.
3:1
Now Solomon made a <u>treaty</u> with Pharaoh, king of Egypt, and married Pharaoh's daughter ; then he brought her to the City of David until he had finished building his own house, and the house of the LORD, and the wall all around Jerusalem.
Definition: agreement, especially of peace, between governments
Synonyms: concord, convention, pact
noun: treaty
Peace **treaties** usually end wars and conflicts.

3:9
"Therefore give to Your servant an understanding heart to judge Your people, that I may <u>discern</u> between good and evil. For who is able to judge this great people of Yours.
Definition: discover with the eyes or mind
Synonyms: see, behold, descry, distinguish, espy, notice, observe, perceive
noun: discerner, discernment
adjective: discernible
verb: discern
adverb: discernibly, discerningly
Strong morals enable us to **discern** between right and wrong.
5:17
And the king commanded them to <u>quarry</u> large stones, costly stones, and hewn stones, to lay the foundation of the temple.
Definition: excavation for obtaining
noun: quarry
An abandoned rock **quarry**, complete with primitive tools, was discovered by archaeologists.
6:3
The <u>vestibule</u> in front of the sanctuary of the house was twenty cubits long across the breadth of the house, and its width extended ten cubits from the front of the house.
Definition: enclosed entrance
Synonyms: foyer, lobby
noun: vestibule
adjective: vestibular
Teenagers are warned not to loiter in front of the **vestibule**.
6:4
And he made for the house windows with <u>beveled</u> frames.
Definition: slant on an edge
Synonyms: diagonal, bevel, bias, biased, slanted, slating
noun: bevel
verb: bevel
Their dream house abounded with **beveled** windows.
7:6
He also made the Hall of Pillars; its length was fifty cubits, and its width thirty cubits; and in front of them was a <u>portico</u> with pillars, and a canopy was in front of them.
Definition: colonnade forming a porch
noun: portico

A portico collapsed while people were standing beneath it.
   7:9
All these were of costly stones, <u>hewn</u> to size, trimmed with saws, inside and out, from the foundation to the <u>eaves</u>, and also on the outside to the great court.
Definition: cut or shape with or as with an ax
noun: hewer
verb: hew
Raw gemstones are hewn to the my specifications.
Definition: overhanging edge of a roof
noun: eaves
His ladder having fallen out from beneath her, the roofer clung precipitously to the **eaves**.
   7:17
He made a <u>lattice</u> network, with wreaths of chainwork, for the capitals which were on top of the pillars; seven chains for one capital and seven for the other capital.
Definition: framework of crossed strips
noun: lattice, latticework
verb: lattice
Dough is laid in a **lattice**-like fashion on the top of a apple pie.
   7:20
The capitals on the two pillars also had pomegranates above, by the <u>convex</u> surface which was next to the network; and there were two hundred such pomegranates in rows on each of the capitals all around.
Definition: curved or rounded like the outside of a sphere
noun: convexity, convexness
adjective: convex
adverb: convexly
The differences between **convex** and concave lenses are studied in a basic physics class.
   7:35
On the top of the cart, at the height of half a cubit, it was perfectly round. And on the top of the cart, its <u>flanges</u> and its panels were of the same casting.
Definition: projecting rim on a wheel, pipe, rail, etc.
noun: flange
Flanges can be used to hold a wheel in place or to strengthen it.
   9:19
all the storage cities that Solomon had, cities for his chariots and cities for his <u>cavalry</u>, and whatever Solomon desired to build in Jerusalem , in Lebanon, and in all the land of his dominion.

Definition: troops on horseback or in vehicles
noun: cavalry, cavalryman
Indian tribes gained several spectacular victories over the U.S. <u>cavalry</u> before finally succumbing to defeat.

10:2
She came to Jerusalem with a very great <u>retinue</u>, with camels that bore spices, very much gold, and precious stones; and when she came to Solomon, she spoke with him about all that was in her heart.
Definition: attendants or followers of a distinguished person
Synonyms: entourage, following, suite, train
noun: retinue
The Queen of England travels with a very large and expensive **retinue**.

16:14
Now the rest of the acts of Elah, and all that he did, are not written in the book of <u>chronicles</u> of the kings of Israel.
Definition: history, record
Synonyms: histories, annals
noun: chronicle, chronicler
verb: chronicle
Chronicles of numerous cultures can be found in a library or on the internet.

18:21
And Elijah came to all the people, and said, "How long will you <u>falter</u> between two opinions? If the LORD is God follow Him; but if Baal, then follow him," But the people answered him not a word.
Definition: more unsteadily
Synonyms: teeter, lurch, stagger, stumble, topple, totter, wobble
noun: falter, falterer
adjective:
verb: falter
adverb: falteringly
Though he came close to a world record in the marathon, the runner **faltered** just a kilometer before the finish line.

18:28
So they cried aloud, and cut themselves, as was in their custom, with knives and <u>lances</u>, until the blood gushed out on them.
Definition: spear
noun: lance, lancer
verb: lance
Unarmed peasants on foot are no match for mounted soldiers carrying **lances**.

18:32
Then with the stones he build an altar in the names of the LORD; and he made a <u>trench</u> around the altar large enough to hold two seahs of seed.
Definition: long, narrow cut in land
Synonyms: cut, ditch
noun: trench
verb: trench
A **trench** was dug around the city to protect its from invading hordes.

20:43
So the king of Israel went to his house <u>sullen</u> and displeased, and came to Samaria.
Definition: gloomily silent; dismal
Synonyms: dour, glum, morose, saturnine, sulky, surly, ugly, crabbed, crabby
noun: sullenness
adjective: sullen
adverb: sullenly
Large numbers of Olympic athletes were **sullen** following their lackluster performances.

KINGS II

KINGS II

KINGS II

9:30
And when Jehu had come to Jezreel, Jezebel heard of it; and she put paint on her eyes and <u>adorned</u> her head, and looked through a window.
Definition: decorate with ornaments
Synonyms: beautified, bedecked, decked, decorated, dressed up, embellished, garnished, ornamented, trimmed
noun: adornment
verb: adorn
A golden tiara **adorned** the head of the princess.

9:32
And he looked up at the window, and said, "Who is on my side? Who? And two or three <u>eunuchs</u> looked out at him.
Definition: castrated man
noun: eunuch
Eunuches once wielded great influence with the emperor of China.

11:7
"The two <u>contingents</u> of you who go off duty on the Sabbath shall keep the watch of the house of the LORD for the king."
Definition: a share, proportion, or quota as of troops, ships, laborers, delegates, etc; a group or body forming part of a larger one
noun: contingent
A **contingent** of troops were sent out to draw enemy forces from the base.

12:5
"let the priests take it themselves, each from his <u>constituency</u>, and let them repair the damages of the temple, wherever any dilapidation is found.
Definition: component; having power to elect
Synonyms: electorate, voter
noun: constituent, constituency
adjective: constituent
adverb: constituently
Politicians are too often beholden to their **constituencies**.

15:20
And Menahem <u>exacted</u> the money from Israel, from all the very wealthy, from each man fifty shekels of silver, to give to the King of Assyria. So the king of Assyria turned back, and did not stay there in the land.
Definition: compel to furnish
Synonyms: extorted, gouged, pinched, screwed, squeezed, wrenched, wrested, wrung
noun: exactingness, exaction, exactitude, exactness, exactor
adjective: exact, exactable, exacting

verb: exact
adverb: exactly
During the revolt, the prisoners **exacted** revenge on their captors.

    17:3

Shalmaneser king of Assyria came up against him; and Hoshea became his vassal, and paid him tribute money.
Definition: one acknowledging another as feudal lord; one in a dependent position
noun: vassal, vassalage
Lesser nations were forced to acknowledge themselves as **vassals** to the Roman empire.

    18:17

Then the king of Assyria sent the Tartan, the Rabsaris, and the Rabshakeh from Lachish, with a great army against Jerusalem, to King Hezekiah. And they went up and came to Jerusalem. When they had come up, they came and stood by the aqueduct from the upper pool, which was on the highway to the Fuller's Field..
Definition: conduit for carrying running water
Synonyms: channel, canal, conduit, course, duct, watercourse
noun: aqueduct
Aqueducts carried water into the city and sewage out of it.

    18:18

And when they had called to the King, Eliakim the son of Hilkiah, who was over the household, Shebna the scribe, and Joah the son of Asaph, the recorder, came out to them.
Definition: one who writes or copies
noun: scribe
verb: scribe
Scribes make **transcripts** of all official court proceedings.

    19:26

Therefore their inhabitants had little power; They were dismayed and confounded; They were as the grass of the field And the green herb, As the grass on the housetops And grain blighted before it is grown.
Definition: confused
Synonyms: aghast, agape, dismayed, dumbfounded, overwhelmed, shocked, puzzled, befogged, bewildered, confused, perplexed, posed, stumbled
noun: confounder
verb: confound
adverb: confoundedly
The riddle of the Sphinx **confounded** those who heard it.

19:28
Because your rage against Me and your tumult Have come up to My ears, Therefore I will put my hook in your nose and my bridle in your lips, And I will turn you back By the way which you came.
Definition: headgear to control a horse
noun: bridle
verb: bridle
Wild horses will refuse to be **bridled.**

21:13
'And I will stretch over Jerusalem the measuring line of Samaria and the plummet of the house of Ahab; I will wipe Jerusalem as one wipes a dish, wiping it and turning it upside down.
Definition: drop straight down
Synonyms: dip, drop, fall, plunge, skid, tumble
verb: plummet
After the sex scandal was made public, the presidential candidate's poll numbers **plummeted.**

Random Review - Kings I & II

Match the numbered words with their lettered definitions. Check your answers in the back of the book.

1.	homage		a.	enclosed entrance
2.	malicious		b.	gloomy
3.	quarry		c.	proportions
4.	vestibule		d.	attendants / followers
5.	flanges		e.	castrated men
6.	retinue		f.	decorated
7.	chronicles		g.	ill will
8.	sullen		h.	in a dependent position
9.	adorned		i.	excavate
10.	contingents		j.	drop straight down
11.	constituency		k.	reverent regard
12.	eunuchs		l.	conduit for carrying water
13.	vassal		m.	history records
14.	aqueduct		n.	having power to elect
15.	plummet		o.	protecting rim

Try These

Use the complete vocabulary list from the specified book to fill in the missing word for each verse.

Kings I

18:21
And Elijah came to all the people, and said, "How long will you _____ between two opinions? If the LORD is God follow Him; but if Baal, then follow him," But the people answered him not a word.

Kings II

15:20
And Menahem _____ the money from Israel, from all the very wealthy, from each man fifty shekels of silver, to give to the King of Assyria. So the king of Assyria turned back, and did not stay there in the land.

CHRONICLES I

CHRONICLES 1

CHRONICLES I
9:29

Some of them were appointed over the furnishings and over all the implements of the sanctuary, and over the fine flour and the wine and the oil and the incense and the spices.

Definition: piece of equipment for performing hand or mechanical operation
Synonyms: instruments, tools, utensils
noun: implement, implementation
verb: implement

Due to the unexpected malfunction of her expensive sewing machine, the seamstress was forced to use her low tech **implements**: a needle and thread.

11:23

And he killed an Egyptian, a man of great height, five cubits tall. In the Egyptian's hand there had been a spear like a weaver's beam; and he went down to him with a staff, wrested the spear out of the Egyptian's hand, and killed him with his own spear.

Definition: pull or move by a forcible twisting movement; gain with difficulty
Synonyms: wrenched, wrung
noun: wrests
verb: wrest

During the coup attempt, the army attempted to **wrest** power from the elected government.

16:4

And he appointed some of the Levites to minister before the ark of the LORD, to commemorate, to thank, and to praise the LORD GOD of Israel:

Definition: celebrate or honor
Synonyms: keep, celebrate, observe, solemnize, memorialize, monumentalize
noun: commemoration, commemorator
adjective: commemorative
verb: commemorate
adverb: commemoratively

In 1976 America **commemorated** its two hundreth anniversary.

CHRONICLES II

CHRONICLES II

6:23
"then hear from heaven, and act, and judge Your servants, bringing <u>retribution</u> on the wicked by bringing his way on his own head, and justifying the righteous by giving him according to his righteousness.
Definition: retaliation
Synonyms: avenging, counterblow, reprisal, requital, revanche, revenge, vengeance
noun: retribution
adjective: retributive, retributory
adverb: retributively
Exacting **retribution** for every offense will create an endless cycle of violence.

15:5
"And in those times there was no peace to the one who went out, nor to the one who came in, but great <u>turmoil</u> was on all the inhabitants of the lands.
Definition: extremely agitated condition
Synonyms: commotion, agitation, confusion, dither, tumult, turbulence, unrest, disquietude, restlessness
noun: turmoil
With the assassination of the president, the small nation was left in **turmoil**.

16:12
And in the thirty-ninth year of his reign, Asa became diseased in his feet, and his <u>malady</u> was very severe; yet in his disease he did not seek the LORD, but the physicians.
Definition: disorder
Synonyms: affliction, ailment, complaint, condition, ill, infirmity, sickness, syndrome
noun: malady
A proper diet, along with exercise, can prevent many **maladies** from occurring.

26:9
And Uzziah built towers in Jerusalem at the Corner Gate, at the Valley Gate, and at the corner <u>buttress</u> of the wall; then he fortified them.
Definition: projecting structure to support a wall; support
Synonyms: brace, column, prop, shore, stay, underpinning
noun: buttress
verb: buttress
NATO would like to use Turkey as a **buttress** against some hostile Middle-Eastern nations.

29:8
"Therefore the wrath of the LORD fell upon Judah and Jerusalem, and He

has given them up to trouble, to astonishment, and to jeering, as you see with your eyes.
Definition: speak or cry out in derision; ridicule
Synonyms: scoffing, flouting, gibing, girding, jesting, quipping at, scouting, sneering
noun: jeer, jeerer
verb: jeer
adverb: jeeringly
An obvious lack of talent caused the would-be stand-up comedian to be **jeered** by the audience.

Random Review - Chronicles I & II

Match the numbered words with their lettered definitions. Check your answers in the back of the book.

1.	implements		a.	extremely agitated condition
2.	wrested		b.	pull with force
3.	commemorate		c.	support
4.	retribution		d.	disorder
5.	turmoil		e.	retaliation
6.	malady		f.	ridicule
7.	buttress		g.	equipment
8.	jeering		h.	honor

Try These

Use the complete vocabulary list from the specified book to fill in the missing word for each verse.

Chronicles I

    11:23
And he killed an Egyptian, a man of great height, five cubits tall. In the Egyptian's hand there had been a spear like a weaver's beam; and he wen down to him with a staff, _____ him the spear out of the Egyptian's hand, and killed him with his own spear.

Chronicles II

    6:23
"then hear from heaven, and act, and judge Your servants, bringing _____ on the wicked by bringing his way on his own head, and justifying the righteous by giving him according to his righteousness.

    16:12
And in the thirty-ninth year of his reign, Asa became diseased in his feet, and his _____ was very severe; yet in his disease he did not seek the LORD, but the physicians.1

EZRA

EZRA

EZRA
    4:15

that search may be made in the book of the records of your fathers. And you will find in the book of the records and know that this city is a rebellious city, harmful to kings and provinces, and that they have <u>incited</u> <u>sedition</u> within the city in former times, for which cause the city was destroyed.

Definition: arouse to action
Synonyms: abetted, fomented, instigated, provoked, raised, set, set on, stirred up, whipped up
noun: incitant, incitation, incitement, inciter
verb: incite

Demagogues **incite** the public by appealing to emotion and prejudice.

Definition: revolution against a government
Synonyms: treason
noun: sedition, seditiousness
adjective: seditious
verb: seditiously

Legally **sedition** is not quite as serious a crime as treason.
    6:11

Also I issue a decree that whoever alters this <u>edict</u>, let a timber be pulled from his house and erected, and let him be hanged on it; and let his house be made a refuse heap because of this.

Definition: decree
Synonyms: directive, ruling, ukase
noun: edict
adjective: edictal

By royal **edict**, taxes were raised by two percent throughout the kingdom.
    7:25

And you, Ezra, according to your God-given wisdom, set <u>magistrates</u> and judges who may judge all the people who are in the region beyond the River, all such as know the laws of your God; and teach those who do not know them.

Definition: judge
Synonyms: courts, justices
noun: magistrate
adjective: magisterial
verb: magisterially

Federal **magistrates** are paid substantially more than state ones.
    7:26

Whoever will not observe the law of your God and the law of the king, let judgement be executed speedily on him, whether it be death, or banishment,

or <u>confiscation</u> of goods, or imprisonment.
Definition: take by authority
Synonyms: secure, take
noun: confiscation, confiscator
adjective: confiscable, confiscatory
verb: confiscate
Imminent domain laws give governments the right to **confiscate** private property so long as compensation is provided.
   8:36
And they delivered the king's orders to the king's <u>satraps</u> and the governors in the region beyond the River. So they gave support to the people and the house of God.
Definition: subordinate ruler
noun: satrap
The conspirators made sure that they killed the **satraps,** as well as the king.
   10:10
Then Ezra the priest stood up and said to them, "You have transgressed and have taken <u>pagan</u> wives, adding to the guilt of Israel.
Definition: heathen
Synonyms: infidel
noun: pagan, paganism
adjective: paganish
verb: paganize
In their infancies, many religions believed that **pagans** should be killed.

NEHEMIAH

NEHEMIAH

4:1

But it so happened, when Sanballat heard that we were rebuilding the wall, that he was furious and very <u>indignant</u>, and mocked the Jews.

Definition: anger aroused by something unjust or unworthy
Synonyms: angry, acrimonious, choleric, heated, irate, ireful, mad, waxy, wrathful
noun: indignation
adjective: indignant
adverb: indignantly

Feeling that she had been wronged by the judges, the figure skater was very **indignant**.

9:19

Yet in Your <u>manifold</u> mercies
You did not forsake them in the wilderness.
The pillar of the cloud did not depart from them by day,
To lead them on the road;
Nor the pillar of fire by night,
To show them light,
And the way they should go.

Definition: marked by diversity or variety
Synonyms: diverse, multifarious, multiform, multiplex
noun: manifold

Once he turned off the television and began to concentrate, **manifold** essay topics came to him.

10:31

that if the peoples of the land bring <u>wares</u> or any grain to sell on the Sabbath day, we would not buy it from them on the Sabbath, or on a holy day; and that we would forego the seventh year's produce and the exaction of every debt.

Definition: articles for sale
Synonyms: merchandise, commodities, goods, line
noun: wares

Without well-developed distribution systems, many Third World farmers and merchants bring their **wares** by hand to the marketplace.

REHEARSAL

1

...when Sarah had heard this, she was furious, not
that he was furious and yet, until night and noon and the...

Definition: her trousers by something unfasten... twisted by
synonyms: angry, acrimonious, choleric, heated, irate, ireful, mad,
waxy, wrathful
noun: indignation
adjective: indignant
adverb: indignantly

Feeling as if she had been virtually twice judged, she lightly/slightly waved
indignant
9.18
Yet in your manifold mercies
You did not forsake them in the wilderness.
The pillar of the cloud did not depart from them by day,
To lead them on the road,
Nor the pillar of fire by night,
To show them light
And the way they should go.

Definition: marked by diversity or variety
Synonyms: diverse, multifarious, multiform, multiplex
noun: manifold

Once he turned off the television and began to concentrate, a manifold essay
was puzzling to him.
10.31
...that the peoples of the land bring wares or any grain to sell on the sabbath
day we would not buy it from them on the sabbath or on a holy day; and
that we would forgo the seventh year's produce and the exaction of every
debt.

Definition: article for sale
Synonyms: merchandise, commodities, goods, lines
noun: wares

Without well-developed distribution systems, many Third World farmers
and merchants bring their wares by hand to the market place.

ESTHER

ESTHER
1:8
In accordance with the law, the drinking was not <u>compulsory</u>; for so the king had ordered all the officers of his household, that they should do according to each man's pleasure.
Definition: coercion
Synonyms: mandatory, imperative, imperious, obligatory, required
noun: compulsion, compulsiveness
adjective: compulsory
adverb: compulsively, compulsorily
If the president were to reinstate the draft, military service would be **compulsory**.

5:13
"Yet all this <u>avails</u> me nothing, so long as I see Mordecai the Jew sitting at the king's gate."
Definition: be of use or make use
Synonyms: benefits, advantages, profits, serves, works for
verb: avail
If you haven't read the chapters and done the assignments by now, cramming before the test will **avail** you nothing.

7:4
"For we have been sold, my people and I, to be destroyed, to be killed, and to be annihilated. Had we been sold as male and female slaves, I would have held my tongue, although the enemy could never <u>compensate</u> for the king's loss."
Definition: offset or balance; repay
Synonyms: atone for, balance, counterbalance, counterpoise, make up, outweigh, redeem, set off
noun: compensation, compensator
adjective: compensational, compensatory
verb: compensate
The government must **compensate** the owners of seized property.

Random Review - Ezra, Nehemiah, & Esther

Match the numbered words with their lettered definitions. Check your answers in the back of the book.

1.	incited		a.	aroused to action
2.	sedition		b.	taken by authority
3.	edict		c.	heathen
4.	magistrates		d.	angered by something unjust
5.	confiscation		e.	decree
6.	satraps		f.	goods
7.	pagan		g.	diverse
8.	indignant		h.	judges
9.	manifold		i.	subordinate ruler
10.	wares		j.	revolution
11.	compulsory		k.	makes use of
12.	compensate		l.	repay
13.	avails		m.	coerced

Try These

Use the complete vocabulary list from the specified book to fill in the missing word for each verse.

Ezra

    4:15
that search may be made in the book of the records of your fathers. And you will find in the book of the records and know that this city is a rebellious city, harmful to kings and provinces, and that they have _____ sedition within the city in former times, for which cause the city was destroyed.

Nehemiah

    4:1
But it so happened, when Sanballat heard that we were rebuilding the wall, that he was furious and very _____, and mocked Jews.

Esther

    5:13
"Yet all this _____ me nothing, so long as I see Mordecai the Jew sitting at the king's gate."

JOB

JOB
1:10
Have you not made a <u>hedge</u> around him, around his household, and around all that he has on every side? You have blessed the work of his hands, and his possessions have increased in the land.
Definition: means of protection
Synonyms: enclose, cage, close in, coop, corral, envelop, fence, hem, immure, mew, pen, shut in, wall
noun: hedge, hedger
adjective: hedge
verb: hedge
Betting some money on both teams, rather than all money on a single team, provides a **hedge** against losing everything.
3:8
May those curse it who curse the day, Those who are ready to arouse a <u>Leviathan</u>.
Definition: large sea animal
Synonyms: giant, behemoth, mammoth, monster, whale
noun: leviathan
adjective: leviathan
The Loch Ness Monster is considered a **leviathan**.
5:24
You shall know that your tent is in peace; You shall visit your habitation and find nothing <u>amiss</u>.
Definition: in the wrong way
Synonyms: astray, awry
adjective: amiss
adverb: amiss
The homeowner knew that something was **amiss** when he arrived home to find that his lock had been forced open.
6:5
Does the wild donkey <u>bray</u> when it has grass, Or does the ox low over its fodder?
Definition: harsh cry of a donkey
noun: bray
verb: bray
Children were warned that the donkey would not only **bray** if its tail were pulled, but would kick as well.
8:3
Does God <u>subvert</u> judgment? Or does the Almighty <u>pervert</u> justice?
Definition: overthrow or ruin

135

Synonyms: sabotage, undermine, wreck
noun: subversion, subversiveness
adjective: subversive
verb: subvert
adverb: subversively
Terrorists attempted to **subvert** foreign governments.
Definition: corrupt or distort
Synonyms: debase, bastardize, brutalize, canker, debauch, demoralize, deprave, vitiate
noun: pervert, perversion, perversiveness
verb: pervert
adverb: pervertedly
As the decades passed the original intent of the legislation was **perverted**.
    8:11
"Can the papyrus grown up without a marsh? Can the reeds flourish without water?
Definition: tall grasslike plant; paper from papyrus
Synonyms: swamp, mire, morass, quagmire
noun: papyrus
Ancient civilizations recorded information on **papyrus**.
Definition: soft, wet land
noun: marsh, marshiness
adjective: marshlike, marshy
The Everglades are replete with **marshes**.
    8:13
So are the paths of all who forget God; And the hope of the hypocrite shall perish,
Definition: a feigning to be what one is not
Synonyms: dissembler, dissimulator, lip server, pharisee, white sepulcher
noun: hypocrisy, hypocrite
adjective: hypocritical
Politicians that advocate strong morals and then become involved in scandals are considered **hypocrites**.
    9:17
For He crushes me with a tempest, And multiplies my wounds without cause.
Definition: violent storm
noun: tempest, tempestuousness
adjective: tempestuous
adverb: tempestuously
A monsoon is a type of **tempest**.

10:11
Clothe me with skin and flesh , And knit me together with bones and <u>sinews</u>?
Definition: tendons
Synonyms: mainstays, backbones, pillars
noun: sinew
adjective: sinewy
Though he did not possess a large body his **sinews** were powerful.

13:12
Your <u>platitudes</u> are proverbs of ashes, Your defenses are defenses of clay.
Definition: trite remark
Synonyms: banalities, bromides, cliches, shibboleths, tags, truisms
noun: platitude
adjective: platitudinously
adverb: platitudinously
Platitudes have been used so often that they no longer hold the meaning that they once did.

14:19
As water wears away stones, And as <u>torrents</u> wash away the soil of the earth; So You destroy the hope of man.
Definition: rushing stream, tumultuous outburst
Synonyms: floods, cataclysms, cataracts, deluges, inundations, overflows, pours, spates
noun: torrent
adjective: torrential
adverb: torrentially
Torrential rains cause destructive floods every year.

16:9
He tears me in His wrath and hates me; He <u>gnashes</u> at me with His teeth; My adversary sharpens His gaze on me.
Definition: grind (as teeth) together
noun: gnash
verb: gnash
Being told that she would not receive the promotion after all caused her to **gnash** her teeth.

16:13
His archers surround me. He pierces my heart and does not pity; He pours out my <u>gall</u> on the ground.
Definition: bile; insolence
noun: gall
verb: gall

It takes **gall** to ask for a raise on the second day on the job.
    19:13
"He has removed my brothers far from me, And my acquaintances are completely <u>estranged</u> from me.
Definition: make hostile
Synonyms: alienated, disaffected, disunited, weaned
noun: estranged
verb: estrange
Estranged couples often reconciled after a time apart.
    21:18
They are like straw before the wind, And like <u>chaff</u> that a storm carries away.
Definition: debris separated from grain; something worthless
Synonyms: banter
noun: chaff
adjective: chaffy
verb: chaff
The under-achieving students were separated from the rest like **chaff** from wheat.
    21:24
His pails are full of milk, And the <u>marrow</u> of his bones is moist,
Definition: soft tissue in the cavity of the bone
Synonyms: essence, pith, quintessence, quintessential, soul, substance, virtuality
noun: marrow
When food was less plentiful, people often ate the **marrow** of bones as well as the meat.
    27:1
Moreover, Job continued his <u>discourse</u>, and said: As God lives who has taken away my justice, And the Almighty.
Definition: conversation; formal treatment of a subject
Synonyms: speech, utterance, verbalization, disquisition, dissertation
noun: discourse
verb: discourse
Public **discourse** is often the best method of problem solving.
    30:6
They had to live in <u>clefts</u> of the valleys, In caves of the earth and the rocks
Definition: cracks
Synonyms: chinks, fissures, rifts, rimes, splits, ravines, arroyos, charns, cloves, gaps, gorges, gulches, schisms, cleavages
noun: cleft
adjective: cleft

Chin **clefts** can be artificially created through surgery.

30:12

At my right hand the rabble arises; They push away my feet, And they raise against me their ways of destruction.

Definition: mob
Synonyms: rout, dregs, masses, other half, proletariat, ragtag, riffraff, scum, scurf, tag and rag, trash
noun: rabble, rabblement
verb: rabble

The **rabble** fled in fear once they realized their intended victims were armed soldiers.

30:19

He has cast me into the mire, And I have become like dust and ashes.

Definition: heavy deep mud
Synonyms: swamp, bog, fen, marsh, morass, quagmire, slough, swampland
noun: mire
verb: mire

Mire trapped the wagons of the settlers thus preventing their forward progress.

31:38

"If my land cries out against me, And its furrows weep together;

Definition: trench made by a plow, wrinkle, or groove
Synonyms: corrugations, creases, crinkles, folds, ridges
noun: furrow
verb: furrow

Seeds were placed into the **furrow** at fourteen inch intervals.

32:13

Lest you say, 'We have found wisdom'; God will vanquish him, not man.

Definition: overcome in battle or in a contest
Synonyms: conquer, bear down, beat down, crush, defeat, overpower, reduce, subdue, subjugate
noun: vanquisher
adjective: vanquishable
verb: vanquish

Though he achieved numerous conquests, Napoleon was finally **vanquished**.

33:20

So that his life abhors bread, And his soul succulent food.

Definition: juicy
Synonyms: sappy
noun: succulence, succulent

adjective: succulent
adverb: succulently
Tender steak appears **succulent** to everyone save vegetarians.
    34:3
For the ear tests words As the palate tastes food.
Definition: roof of the mouth
Synonyms: taste
noun: palate
adjective: palatal
adverb: palatally
Though the new dish had been thought to be novel, it offended the palate of the food critic.
    34:31
"For has anyone said to God, "I have borne chastening; I will offend no more;
Definition: discipline
Synonyms: punishing, castigating, chastising, correcting, disciplining
noun: chastener, chastenment
verb: chasten
Unruly children desperately need to be **chastened**.
    38:9
When I made the clouds its garment, And thick darkness its swaddling band;
Definition: bind (an infant) in bands of cloth
Synonyms: swathing, draping, enveloping, enwrapping
verb: swaddle
New **swaddling** garments were provided for the infant.
    39:28
It dwells on the rock, and resides On the crag of the rock and the stronghold.
Definition: steep cliff
noun: crag
adjective: craggy
Mountain goats are skilled at negotiating **crags**.

Random Review - Job

Match the numbered words with their lettered definitions. Check your answers in the back of the book.

1. Leviathan
2. amiss
3. bray
4. futile
5. pervert
6. subvert
7. tempest
8. sinews
9. platitudes
10. chaff
11. palate
12. swaddling
13. crag
14. succulent
15. furrows

a. tendons
b. wrong way
c. corrupt
d. debris from grain
e. band of cloth
f. trenches
g. large sea animal
h. roof of mouth
i. steep cliff
j. donkey's cry
k. violent storm
l. juicy
m. ruin
n. trite remarks
o. useless

Try These

Use the complete vocabulary list from the specified book to fill in the missing word for each verse.

Job

8:13
So are the paths of all who forget God; And the hope of the _____ shall perish,

19:13
"He has removed my brothers far from me, And my acquaintances are completely _____ from me.

PSALMS

PSALMS
13:6
I will sing to the LORD,
Because He has dealt <u>bountifully</u> with me.
Definition: generosity; reward
Synonyms: plentifully, abundantly, copiously, liberally, bounteously, freely, freehandly, generously, handsomely, munificently, openhandedly, unsparingly
noun: bounty, bounteousness, bountifulness
adjective: bounteous, bountiful
adverb: bounteously, bountifulness
Thanks to excellent weather conditions this season, the harvest will be a **bountiful** one.

17:2
Let my <u>vindication</u> come from Your presence;
Definition: avenge; exonerate; justify
noun: vindication, vindicator
verb: vindicate
The conspiracy uncovered, the defendant was **vindicated** by the dismissal of the trial.

27:5
For in the time of trouble
He shall hide me in His <u>pavilion</u>;
In the secret place of His tabernacle
He shall hide me;
He shall set me high upon a rock.
Definition: large tent; light structure used for entertainment
noun: pavilion
People often bond with their neighbors at summer concerts in the local **pavilion**.

34:18
The LORD is near to those who have a broken heart,
And saves such as have a <u>contrite</u> spirit.
Definition: repentant
Synonyms: remorseful, apologetic, compunctious, penitent, penitential, regretful, repentant, sorry
noun: contriteness, contrition
adjective: contrite
adverb: contritely
Sincere **contriteness** can defuse a damaging situation.

44:13
You make us a reproach to our neighbors,
A scorn and <u>derision</u> to those around us.
Definition: make fun of
Synonyms: laughingstock, butt, jest, joke, mock, mockery, sport
noun: derider, derision, derisiveness
adjective: derisive
verb: deride
adverb: deridingly, derisively
People are often **derided** for being different.

48:13
Mark well her <u>bulwarks</u>;
Consider her palaces;
That you may tell it to the generation following.
Definition: wall-like defense
Synonyms: bastions, breastworks, parapets, ramparts
noun: bulwark
verb: bulwark
Berlin's former wall acted as a **bulwark** against Western influence.

49:4
I will incline my ear to a proverb;
I will <u>disclose</u> my dark saying on the harp.
Definition: reveal
Synonyms: open, display, expose, unclothe, uncover, unveil
noun: discloser, disclosure
verb: disclose
Full disclosure is legally mandated for government entities.

66:17
I cried to Him with my mouth,
And He was <u>extolled</u> with my tongue.
Definition: praise highly
Synonyms: blessed, celebrated, eulogized, glorified, hymned, lauded, magnified, resounded
noun: extoller
verb: extol
Religious leaders frequently **extol** the virtues of generosity and sacrifice.

68:31
<u>Envoys</u> come out of Egypt;
Ethiopia will quickly stretch out her hands to God.
Definition: diplomat
Synonyms: extraordinary, minister, plenipotentiary

noun: envoy
A State Department **envoy** was sent to help defuse the political strife.
    75:8
For in the hand of the LORD there is a cup,
And the wine is red;
It is fully mixed, and He pours it out;
Surely its <u>dregs</u> shall all the wicked of the earth
Drain and drink down.
Definition: most worthless part
Synonyms: rabble, masses, mob, other half, proletariat, ragtag and bobtail, riffraff, rout, scum, scurf, tag and rag, trash
noun: dreg
Some consider criminals and the unemployed to be the **dregs** of society.
    85:8
I will hear what God the LORD will speak,
For He will speak peace
To his people and to his saints;
But let them not turn back to <u>folly</u>.
Definition: foolishness
Synonyms: absurdity, craziness, inanity, insanity, lunacy, lunacy, preposterousness, senselessness
noun: folly
Though people said that it was **folly** to attempt to fly, the Wright brothers tried to regardless.
88:15
I have been afflicted and ready to die from my mouth up;
I suffer Your terrors;
I am <u>distraught</u>.
Definition: agitated with mental conflict
Synonyms: distrait, distressed, harassed, tormented, troubled, worried
adjective: distraught
adverb: distraughtly
The senseless murder of his family left him **distraught** and suicidal.
    101:5
Whoever secretly slanders his neighbors,
Him I will destroy;
The one who has a <u>haughty</u> look and a proud heart,
Him I will not endure.
Definition: disdainfully proud
Synonyms: proud, arrogant, cavalier, disdainful, dismissive, hubristic, huffy, insolent, lofty, lordly, overbearing

noun: haughtiness
adjective: haughty
verb: haughtily
Self-confidence is an asset but **haughtiness** is a liability.

    106:23
Therefore He said that He would destroy them,
Had not Moses His chosen one stood before Him in the <u>breach</u>,
To turn away His wrath, lest He destroy them.
Definition: breaking of a law, obligation, standard
Synonyms: break, fissure, fracture, infraction, rift, rupture, schism, transgression, trespass, violation
noun: breach
verb: breach
Betrayal is perhaps the worst **breach** of trust between friends.

    117:1
Oh, praise the LORD, all you Gentiles!
<u>Laud</u> Him, all you peoples!
Definition: praise
Synonyms: bless, celebrate, eulogize, glorify, hymn, laud, magnify, psalm, psalmody, resound
noun: laud, laudability, laudableness, laudation
adjective: laudable, laudatory
verb: laud
adverb: laudably
His friends and family **lauded** his recovery from drug and alcohol addictions.

    119:96
I have seen the <u>consummation</u> of all perfection,
But Your commandment is exceedingly broad.
Definition: complete or perfect
noun: consumption, consumptive
adjective: consumptive
adverb: consumptively
Even under the most stressing of circumstances, she was the **consummate** hostess.

    119:119
You put away all of the wicked of the earth like <u>dross</u>;
Definition: waste matter
noun: dross
adjective: drossy
Much **dross** marked the trail that the herd had taken.

137:7
Remember, O LORD, against the sons of Edom
The day of Jerusalem,
Who said, "Raze it, raze it,
To its very foundation!"
Definition: destroy or tear down
Synonyms: destroy, annihilate, atomize, decapitate, demolish, destruct, dismantle, dissolve, dynamite
verb: raze
Local governments are **razing** high rise housing developments and replacing them with townhouses.

140:3
They sharpen their tongues like a serpent;
The poison of asps is under their lips.
Definition: poisonous African snake
noun: asps
The herpetologist failed to heed his own advice and was bitten by an **asp**.

143:5
I remember the days of old;
I meditate on all Your works;
I muse on the work of Your hands.
Definition: ponder
Synonyms: deliberate, meditate, mull over, ruminate
verb: muse
Only the most highly desired college graduates have the opportunity to **muse** over their job offers.

Random Review - Psalms

Match the numbered words with their lettered definitions. Check your answers in the back of the book.

1.	bountifully	a.	most worthless parts
2.	vindication	b.	very poor
3.	pavilion	c.	rules of conduct
4.	bulwarks	d.	walls of defense
5.	extolled	e.	praise
6.	envoys	f.	proud
7.	dregs	g.	with generosity
8.	haughty	h.	completion
9.	destitute	i.	waste matter
10.	breach	j.	exoneration
11.	precepts	k.	tear down
12.	laud	l.	praise highly
13.	consummation	m.	break down
14.	dross	n.	tent
15.	raze	o.	diplomats

Try These

Use the complete vocabulary list from the specified book to fill in the missing word for each verse.

Psalms

17:2
Let my _____ come from Your presence;

66:17
I cried to Him with my mouth,
And He was _____ with my tongue.

PROVERBS

PROVERBS

1:6
To understand a proverb and an <u>enigma</u>,
The words of the wise and their riddles.
Definition: puzzle or mystery
Synonyms: Chinese puzzle, closed book, conundrum, mystification, puzzle, puzzlement, riddle, why
noun: enigma
adjective: enigmatic
adverb: enigmatically
Prophecies are usually **enigmatic** and subject to multiple interpretations.

1:21
She cries out in the chief <u>concourses</u>,
At the openings of the gates in the city
She speaks her words:
Definition: open space where crowds gather
Synonyms: gatherings, junctions, meetings
noun: concourse
At lunchtime the underground **concourse** of the Pentagon is usually crowded.

1:32
For the turning away of the simple will slay them,
And the <u>complacency</u> of fools will destroy them:
Definition: self-satisfaction
Synonyms: conceit, amour propre, complacence, consequence, egoism, egotism, narcissism, pride, swelled
noun: complacence, complacency
adjective: complacent
adverb: complacently
Complacency will often lead to failure in most endeavors.

5:19
As a loving deer and a graceful <u>doe</u>,
Let her breasts satisfy you at all times;
And always be enraptured with her love.
Definition: adult female deer
noun: doe, doeskin
While tracking a **doe**, the hunter accidentally shot another hunter.

6:6
Go to the ant, you <u>sluggard</u>!
Consider her ways and be wise.
Definition: habitually lazy person

Synonyms: bum, do-nothing, idler, loafer, slouch, slug
noun: sluggard
adjective: sluggardly
Lacking enthusiasm about the work, he performed his task **sluggardly**.
    6:23
For the commandment is a lamp,
And the law is light;
<u>Reproofs</u> of instruction are the way of life,
Definition: blame or censure for a fault
Synonyms: rebukes, admonishments, admonitions, raps, reprimands, reproaches, wigs
noun: reproof
Her parents **reproved** her for habitually lying to them.
    6:25
Do not lust after her beauty in your heart,
Nor let her <u>allure</u> you with her eyelids.
Definition: attract
Synonyms: bewitch, captivate, charm, draw, enchant, fascinate, magnetize, take, vile
noun: allure, allurement
verb: allure
adverb: alluringly
Allured by the smell of freshly baked pastry, she dropped what she was doing and raced for the kitchen.
    10:10
He who winks with the eye causes trouble,
But a <u>prating</u> fool will fall.
Definition: talk long and foolishly
Synonyms: chatting, babbling, burbling, cackling, chattering, clacking, clattering, dithering, gabbing, jawing, pattering
noun: prate
adverb pratingly
Nervousness made him **prate** like a child.
    13:12
Hope <u>deferred</u> makes a heart sick,
But when desire comes it is the tree of life.
Definition: postpone
Synonyms: adjourned, delayed, held off, held over, held up, intermitted, laid over, postponed, prorogued, put off, put over, remitted, shelved, stood over, stayed, suspended, waived
noun: deferment, deferral, deferrer, deference

adjective: deferrable, deferent, deferential,
verb: defer
adverb: deferentially
People are always trying to **defer** mandatory jury duty.
    27:22
Though you grind a fool in mortar with a pestle along with crushed grain,
Yet his foolishness will not depart from him.
Definition: strong bowl
Definition: implement for grinding substances in a mortar
noun: mortar
noun: pestle
A group of alchemists feverishly ground herbs into powder using a **mortar** and **pestle** as part of a futile attempt to change lead to gold.
    30:10
Do not malign a servant to his master,
Lest he curse you , and you be found guilty.
Definition: wicked
Synonyms: asperse, bespatter, blacken, calumniate, defame, denigrate, libel, scandalize, slander, slur, smear, spatter, tear down, traduce, vilify
adjective: malign
verb: malignant
adverb: malignly
Serial killers are considered a societal **malignancy.**

Random Review - Proverbs

Match the numbered words with their lettered definitions. Check your answers in the back of the book.

1. enigma
2. concourses
3. complacency
4. sluggard
5. reproof
6. allure
7. transverse
8. prating
9. mortar
10. malign

a. blame
b. lazy person
c. lying across
d. open spaces
e. talk long and foolishly
f. strong bowl
g. puzzle
h. speak wickedly of
i. attract
j. self-satisfaction

Try These

Use the complete vocabulary list from the specified book to fill in the missing word for each verse.

Proverbs

1:6
To understand a proverb and an _____,
The words of the wise and their riddles.

6:25
Do not lust after her beauty in your heart,
Nor let her _____ you with her eyelids.

ECCLESIASTES

ECCLESIASTES

5:20

For he will not dwell <u>unduly</u> on the days of his life, because God keeps him busy with the joy of his heart.

Definition: excessive
Synonyms: ever, confoundedly, consumedly, excessively, extremely, immensely, inordinately, over, overly, super, too
adjective: undue
adverb: unduly

You should not be **unduly** concerned about your failure to make the team.

7:7

Surely oppression destroys a wise man's reason,
And a bribe <u>debases</u> the heart.

Definition: disparage
Synonyms: humbles, abases, casts down, degrades, demeans, humiliates, lowers, sinks
noun: debasement, debaser
verb: debase

She **debased** her husband by marrying another woman.

10:1

Dead flies <u>putrefy</u> the performer's ointment,
And cause it to give off a foul odor;
So does a little folly to one respected for wisdom and honor.

Definition: make or become putrid
Synonyms: decay, break down, corrupt, crumble, decompose, disintegrate, molder, rot, spoil, taint, turn
noun: putrefaction
adjective: putrefactive
verb: putrefy

By not harvesting the fruit from his trees, the farmer allowed it to **putrefy**.

10:4

If the spirit of the ruler rises against you,
Do not leave your post;
For <u>conciliation</u> pacifies great offenses.

Definition: gain the goodwill of
noun: conciliation
adjective: conciliative, conciliatory
verb: conciliate

The ambassador's **conciliatory** tone gave hope that the war could be ended.

12:12

And further, my son, be <u>admonished</u> by these. Of making many books there

is no end, and much study is wearisome to the flesh.
Definition: rebuke
Synonyms: reproved, called, chided, lessoned, rebuked, reprimanded, reproached, ticked off
noun: admonishment, admonition
adjective: admonitory
adverb: admonishingly
verb: admonish
An **admonishing** look immediately quieted the unruly children.

SONG OF SOLOMON

SONG OF SOLOMON

1:9
I have compared you, my love,
To my filly among Pharaoh's chariots.
Definition: young female horse
noun: filly
Considering she's won five consecutive races, It would be wise to bet on that **filly**.

6:11
I went down to the garden of nuts
To see the verdure of the valley,
To see whether the vine had budded
And the pomegranates had bloomed.
Definition: green growing vegetation of its color
Synonyms: foliage, leafage
noun: verdure
adjective: verdurous
Machetes are needed to cut through the thick **verdure** of the Brazilian rain forest.

7:2
Your navel is a rounded goblet
Which lacks no blended beverage.
Your waist is a heap of wheat
Set about with lilies.
Definition: large stemmed drinking glass
noun: goblet
A cache of fifteenth century golden **goblets** was recently discovered.

8:6
Set me as a seal upon your heart,
As a seal upon your arm;
For love is as strong as death,
Jealously as cruel as the grave;
Its flames are flames of fire,
A most vehement flame.
Definition: showing strong especially violent feeling
Synonyms: intense, concentrated, desperate, exquisite, fierce, furious, terrible, vicious, violent
noun: vehemence
adjective: vehement
adverb: vehemently
All of the defendants have **vehemently** denied that they are culpable.

8:14
Make haste, my beloved,
And be like a gazelle
Or a young <u>stag</u>
On the mountains of spices.
Definition: male deer
noun: stag
adjective: stag
During mating season **stags** will fight over a doe.

Random Review - Ecclesiastes & Song of Solomon

Match the numbered words with their lettered definitions. Check your answers in the back of the book.

1. unduly
2. debases
3. putrefy
4. conciliation
5. admonished
6. verdure
7. goblet
8. vehement
9. stag
10. filly

a. gain the goodwill of
b. green vegetation
c. young female horse
d. make putrid
e. male deer
f. strong feeling
g. disparage
h. large stemmed drinking glass
i. rebuked
j. excessive

Try These

Use the complete vocabulary list from the specified book to fill in the missing word for each verse.

Ecclesiastes

10:1
Dead flies _____ the performer's ointment,
And cause it to give off a foul odor;
So does a little folly to one respected for wisdom and honor.

Song of Solomon

8:6
Set me as a seal upon your heart,
As a seal upon your arm;
For love is as strong as death,
Jealously as cruel as the grave;
Its flames are flames of fire,
A most _____ flame.

ISAIAH

ISAIAH

1:4

Alas, sinful nation, A people laden with iniquity, A <u>brood</u> of evildoers, Children who are corrupters! They have forsaken the LORD, They have provoked to anger The Holy One of Israel, They have turned away backward.

Definition: family of young
Synonyms: offspring, children, progeny, issue, posterity, descendants, scions, seed
noun: brood, brooder
adjective: brood
verb: brood
adverb: broodingly

A **brood** of robins was found nesting on the roof.

1:9

Unless the LORD of hosts Had left to us a very small <u>remnant</u>, We would have become like Sodom, We would have been made like Gomorrah.

Definition: small part or trace remaining
Synonyms: remainder, balance, heel, leavings, remains, residual, residue, residuum, rest
noun: remnant
adjective: remnant

Only a **remnant** of World War I veterans remains alive.

1:25

I will turn My hand against you, And thoroughly <u>purge</u> away your dross, And take all your <u>alloy</u>.

Definition: metals fused together
Synonyms: admixture, adulterant, denaturant, amalgam, amalgamation, blend, composite, compound, compost, fusion, immixture
noun: alloy
verb: alloy

With the metals **alloyed**, it was impossible to distinguish them visually.

Definition: purify from
Synonyms: disabuse
noun: purge, purgation, purgative, purger
adjective: purgative
verb: purge
adverb: purgatively

To remove the virus, all computer systems will have to be **purged**.

1:27

Zion shall be redeemed with justice, and her <u>penitents</u> with righteousness.

Definition: feeling sorrow for sins or offense
noun: penitent, penitence
adjective: penitent, penitential
adverb: penitentially, penitently
Penitents can go to confession at a Catholic church.

1:31

The strong shall be as <u>tinder</u>, And the work of it as a spark; Both will burn together, And no one shall quench them.
Definition: substance used to start a fire
Synonyms: kindling
noun: tinder

Lacking a flint, we had to ignite the **tinder** by rubbing two branches against each other.

2:22

<u>Sever</u> yourselves from such a man, Whose breath is in his nostrils; For of what account is he?
Definition: cut off or apart
Synonyms: separate, break up, dichotomize, disjoint, dissect, dissever, disunite, divide, divorce, part, rupture, split up, sunder
noun: severance
adjective: severable
verb: sever

The guillotine **severed** the condemned prisoners head from his body.

3:16

Moreover the LORD says: "Because the daughters of Zion are haughty, And walk with outstretched necks and <u>wanton</u> eyes. Walking and mincing as they go, Making a jingling with their feet.
Definition: excessively merry; lewd
Synonyms: fast, easy, light, loose
noun: wanton, wantonness
adjective: wanton
verb: wanton
adverb: wantonly

Taking their **wantonness** to an extreme, the drunken college students were arrested for disturbing the peace.

3:21

and the rings; The nose jewels the <u>festal</u> apparel and the mantles; The outer garments, the purses
Definition: festive
adjective: festal

Festal costumes are worn during Mardi Gras.
   5:6
I will lay it waste; It shall not be pruned or dug, But there shall come up <u>briers</u> and thorns, I will also command the clouds That they rain no rain on it."
Definition: thorny plant
noun: brier
adjective: briery
Their clothes were torn by running through a **brier** patch.
   5:14
Therefore Sheol has enlarged itself And opened its mouth beyond measure; Their Glory and their multitude and their <u>pomp</u> and he who is jubilant, shall descend into it.
Definition: brilliant display; ostentation
Synonyms: array, fanfare, panoply, parade, shine, show
noun: pomp
Unbelievably, this years celebration contained more **pomp** than lasts.
   7:15
"<u>Curds</u> and honey He shall eat, that He may know to refuse the evil and choose the good.
Definition: coagulated milk
Synonyms: curdles
noun: curd
adjective: curdy
Curdy milk is usually sour.
   7:25
And to any hill which could be dug with the <u>hoe</u>, You will not go there for fear of briers and thorns; But it will become a range for oxen And a place for sheep to roam.
Definition: long-handled tool for cultivating or weeding
noun: hoe
verb: hoe
These days **hoes** are used only by recreational gardeners.
   9:18
For wickedness burns as the fire; It shall devour the briers and thorns, And <u>kindle</u> in the thickets of the forest; They shall mount up like rising smoke.
Definition: set on fire or start burning; stir up
Synonyms: light, enkindle, fire, ignite, inflame , stir, arose, awaken, bestir, rally, rouse, wake, waken, whet
noun: kindle
verb: kindle
That pile of **kindle** unexpectedly erupted with flame.

10:27

It shall come to pass in that day That his burden will be taken away from your shoulder, And his <u>yoke</u> from your neck, And the yoke will be destroyed because of the anointing oil.

Definition: neck frame for coupling draft animals or for carrying loads; clamp; slavery; tie or link; piece of a garment especially at the shoulder
noun: yoke
verb: yoke
Several **yoked** oxen were pulling a plow.

14:27

For the LORD of hosts has purposed, And who will <u>annul</u> it? His hand is stretched out, And who will turn it back.

Definition: make legally void
Synonyms: erase, blackout, blot out, cancel, delete, effaced, expunged, obliterate, wipe out, abolish, abate, abrogate, annihilate, invalidate, negate, nullify, quash, undo, vitiate
noun: annulment
verb: annul
After sixth months of unhappy marriage, the couple had it **annulled**.

16:7

Therefore Moab shall wail for Moab; Everyone shall <u>wail</u>. For the foundations of Kir Hareseth you shall mourn; Surely they are stricken.

Definition: mourn; make a sound like a mournful cry
Synonyms: cry, blubber, sob, weep, howl, bay, quest, ululate, bawl, howl, squall, yowl, complain, fuss, murmur, whine, repine
noun: wail
verb: wail
Plaintive **wails** from the mental institution saddened those who were listening.

17:4

"In that day it shall come to pass That the glory of Jacob will <u>wane,</u> And the fatness of his flesh grow lean.

Definition: grow smaller or less; lose power, prosperity, or influence
Synonyms: abate, ebb, fall, lull, moderate, relent, slacker, subside
noun: wane
verb: wane
The moon waxes and **wanes** during its phases of each month.

22:11

You also made a <u>reservoir</u> between the two walls For the water of the old pool. But you did not look to its Maker, Nor did you have respect for Him who fashioned it long ago.

Definition: place where something (as water) is kept in store
Synonyms: reserve, hoard, inventory, nest egg, stock, stockpile, store
noun: reservoir
Two people drowned in the **reservoir** within the past two months causing the city council to order a higher fence constructed around it..
    22:16
"What have you here, and whom gave you here, That you have hewn a sepulcher here, As he who <u>hewn</u> himself a <u>sepulcher</u> on high, Who carves a tomb for himself in a rock?
Definition: cut or shape with or as with an ax; conform strictly
Synonyms: felled, chopped, cut
noun: hewer
verb: hew
In the garden trees had been **hewn** to the artist's specifications.
Definition: burial suit
Synonyms: grave, burial, tomb
noun: sepulcher
adjective: sepulcher
verb: sepulcher
Only members of the royal family are entombed in the **sepulcher**.
    23:17
And it shall be, at the end of seventy years, that the LORD will visit Tyre. She will return to her pay, and commit <u>fornication</u> with all the kingdoms of the world on the face of the earth.
Definition: illicit sexual intercourse
noun: fornication, fornicator
verb: fornicate
Fornication is grounds for divorce.
    28:5
In that day the LORD of hosts will be For a crown of glory and a <u>diadem</u> of beauty To the remnant of His people.
Definition: crown
noun: diadem
Wearing the **diadem** identified her as a queen.
    30:33
For the Toophet was established of old, Yes, for the king it is prepared. He has made it deep and large; Its <u>pyre</u> is fire with much wood; The breath of the LORD, like a stream of brimstone, kindles it.
Definition: material heaped for a funeral fire
noun: pyre
Vikings destroyed corpses of heroes on funeral **pyres**.

33:19
You will not see a fierce people, A people of <u>obscure</u> speech, beyond perception, Of a stammering tongue that you cannot understand.
Definition: dim or hazy; not well known; vague
Synonyms: dark, dim, dun, dusk, dusky, gloomy, murky, somber, ambiguous, opaque, uncertain, unintelligence, faint, blear, indistinct, adumbrate, obfuscate
noun: obscureness, obscurity
adjective: obscure
verb: obscure
adverb: obscurely
After laboring for years in **obscurity**, the scientist finally achieved a breakthrough.

38:21
Now Isaiah had said, "Let them take a lump of figs, and apply it as a <u>poultice</u> on the boil, and he shall recover."
Definition: warm medicated dressing
noun: poultice
verb: poultice
A **poultice** placed on the wound is only a temporary solution.

40:12
Who has measured the waters in the hollow of his hand, Measured heaven with a <u>span</u> and calculated the dust of the earth in a measure? Weighed the mountains in scales And the hills in a balance.
Definition: amount of time; distance between supports
Synonyms: term, duration, time
noun: span
verb: span
Construction of the monument **spanned** several decades.

43:17
Who brings fourth the chariot and horse, The army and the power (They shall lie down together, they shall not rise; They are <u>extinguished</u>, they are quenched like a <u>wick</u>):
Definition: put out (as a fire)
Synonyms: douse, outed, put out, quenched
noun: extinguisher, extinguishment
adjective: extinguishable
verb: extinguish
Fire-fighters managed to **extinguish** the blaze quickly.
Definition: cord that draws up oil, tallow, or wax to be burned
noun: wick

Cut away some of the candlewax so that the **wick** will be extended.
    47:3
Your nakedness shall be uncovered, Yes, your shame will be seen; I will take <u>vengeance</u>, And I will not <u>arbitrate</u> with a man."
Definition: punishment in retaliation for an injury or offense
Synonyms: retaliation, avenging, reprisal, requital, retribution, revanche, revenge
noun: vengeance
Decades after the end of the war, many soldiers were still consumed with thoughts of **vengeance**.
Definition: settle a dispute as arbitrator
Synonyms: judge, adjudge, adjudicate, referee, umpire
noun: arbitration
adjective: arbitrable
verb: arbitrate
Management and union leaders agreed to go to **arbitration**.
    47:13
You are wearied in the multitude of your counsels; Let now the astrologers, the stargazers, and the monthly <u>prognosticators</u> Stand up and save you From these things
that come upon you.
Definition: predict from signs or symptoms
Synonyms: prophets, augurs, forecasters, foreseers, foretellers, predictors, prophesiers, seers, soothsayers
noun: prognostication, prognosticator
adjective: prognosticative
verb: prognosticate
With amazing skills of **prognostication**, she predicted the Super Bowl score exactly.

    49:1
"Listen, O coastlines, to Me, And take heed, you peoples from afar! The LORD has called Me from the womb; From the <u>matrix</u> of My mother He has made mention of My name.
Definition: something within which something else develops or originates; mold
noun: matrix
 Fetuses can be grown into embryos within a **matrix**.
    52:14
Just as many were astonished at you, So His <u>visage</u> was marred more than any man, And His form more than the sons of men;

Definition: face
Synonyms: countenance, features, look, expression
noun: visage
adjective: visaged
Hatred and contempt expressed on her **visage** made words unnecessary.
54:12
I will make your pinnacles of rubies, Your gates of crystal, And all your walls of precious stones.
Definition: highest point
Synonyms: apexes, acmes, apogees, climaxes, crests, crescendos, crowns, culminations, meridians
noun: pinnacle
Having reached the **pinnacle** of her athletic career, the hurdler retired so that she would always be remembered as a champion.
59:16
He saw that there was no man And wondered that there was no intercessor; Therefore His own arm brought salvation for Him; And his own righteousness, it sustained Him.
Definition: act of reconcile
Synonyms: broker, interceder, intermediary, mediator, middleman, go-between
noun: interceder, intercession, intercessor
adjective: intercessional, intercessory
verb: intercede
United Nations peacekeeping forces **interceded** in the Balkan war.

Random Review - Isaiah

Match the numbered words with their lettered definitions. Check your answers in the back of the book.

1.	brood	a.	small part
2.	remnant	b.	festive
3.	penitent	c.	predictors from signs
4.	tinder	d.	burial suit
5.	wanton	e.	ostentation
6.	festal	f.	illicit sex
7.	pomp	g.	warm medicated dressing
8.	annul	h.	feeling sorrow from sin
9.	sepulcher	i.	funeral fire
10.	fornication	j.	broken piece
11.	diadem	k.	family of young
12.	shard	l.	crown
13.	pyre	m.	lewd
14.	poultice	n.	make legally void
15.	prognosticators	o.	substance used to start fires
16.	matrix	p.	face
17.	visage	q.	one who reconciles
18.	pinnacles	r.	cord for burning
19.	intercessor	s.	highest points
20.	wick	t.	mold

Try These

Use the complete vocabulary list from the specified book to fill in the missing word for each verse.

Isaiah

10:27
It shall come to pass in that day That his burden will be taken away from your shoulder, And his yoke from your neck, And the _____ will be destroyed because of the anointing oil.

14:27
For the LORD of hosts has purposed, And who will _____ it? His hand is stretched out, And who will turn it back.

JEREMIAH

JEREMIAH

1:5
"Before I formed you in the womb I knew you; Before you were born I sanctified you; And I <u>ordained</u> you a prophet to the nations."
Definition: admit to the clergy; decreed
noun: ordainment
verb: ordain
Women are not generally **ordained** as Catholic priests.

2:21
Yet I had planted you a noble vine, a seed of highest quality. How then have you turned before Me Into the <u>degenerate</u> plant of an alien vine?
Definition: degraded or corrupt
Synonyms: decadent, vicious, depraved, flagitious, infamous, miscreant, nefarious, perverse, putrid, rotten
noun: degenerate, degeneracy, degenerately, degeneration
adjective: degenerate, degenerative
verb: degenerate
adverb: degenerately
Lack of physical activity caused his muscles to **degenerate** to the point where he could no longer stand.

2:22
For though you wash yourself with <u>lye</u>, and use much soap, Yet your iniquity is marked before Me," says the LORD God.
Definition: corrosive alkaline substance
noun: lye
Lye is an component of some soaps.

2:23
"How can you say, "I am not polluted, I have not gone after the Baals'? See your way in the valley; Know what you have done: You are a swift <u>dromedary</u> breaking loose in her ways,
Definition: speedy one-humped camel
noun: dromedary
A new **dromedary** has arrived at the city zoo.

3:13
Only acknowledge your <u>iniquity</u>, That you have <u>transgressed</u> against the LORD your God, And have scattered your charms To alien deities under every green tree, And you have not obeyed My voice,' says the LORD.
Definition: wickedness
Synonyms: evil, crime, sin, tort, wrong, wrongdoing
Definition: sinned
Synonyms: violated, breached, contravened, infringed, offended

noun: iniquity, iniquitousness
adjective: iniquitous
adverb: iniquitously
noun: transgression, transgressor
adjective: transgressive
verb: transgress
During Prohibition, **iniquitous** crime families were punished for their **transgressions** against society.

4:7

The lion has come up from his thicket, And the destroyer of nations is on his way. He has gone forth from his place To make your land <u>desolate</u>. Your cities will be laid waste, Without inhabitant.
Definition: lifeless; disconsolate
Synonyms: derelict, abandoned, deserted, forsaken, solitary
noun: desolater, desolation
adjective: desolate,
verb: desolate
adverb: desolately
Our moon has a **desolate** landscape.

9:4

"Everyone take heed to his neighbor, And do not trust any brother; For every brother will utterly <u>supplant</u>, And every Neighbor will walk with slanders.
Definition: take the place of
Synonyms: cut out, displace, usurp, replace, supersede
noun: supplantation, supplanter
verb: supplant
Integrated circuits **supplanted** transistors in the third computer generation.

11:7

"For I earnestly <u>exhorted</u> your fathers in the day that I brought them up out of the land of Egypt, until this day, rising early and exhorting, saying "Obey My voice."
Definition: urge earnestly
Synonyms: urged, egged on, goaded, pricked, prodded, prompted, propelled
noun: exhortation, exhorter
verb: exhort
During his visit to their school, the politician **exhorted** the students to do their best.

11:19

But I was like a <u>docile</u> lamb brought to the slaughter; and I did not know that they had devised schemes against me, saying, "Let us destroy the tree with

its fruit, and let us cut him off from the land of the living, that his name may be remembered no more."
Definition: easily managed
Synonyms: obedient, amenable, biddable, tractable
noun: docility
adjective: docile
adverb: docility
Domesticated house cats are much more **docile** than mountain lions.

    11:23

'and there will be no remnant of them, for I will bring catastrophe on the men of Anathoth, even the year of their punishment.' "
Definition: great disaster or misfortune; utter failure
Synonyms: calamity, cataclysm, misadventure, tragedy, woes
noun: catastrophe
adjective: catastrophic
adverb: catastrophically
Their plan to reopen the old theater proved to be financially **catastrophic**.

    22:14

Who says, "I will build myself a wide house with spacious chambers, And cut out windows for it, Paneling it with cedar And painting it with vermilion.'
Definition: vivid reddish orange
noun: vermilion
Vermillion is a favorite color of many artists.

    24:9

I will deliver them to trouble into all the kingdoms of the earth, for their harm, to be a reproach and a byword, a taunt and a curse, in all places where I shall drive them.
Definition: sarcastic challenge or insult
Synonyms: ridicule, deride, lout, mock, quiz, rally, scout, twit
noun: taunt, taunter
verb: taunt
adverb: tauntingly
Taunting your opponents will result in a technical foul.

    31:14

I will satiate the soul of the priests with abundance, And all my people shall be satisfied with My goodness," says the LORD.
Definition: satisfy fully; surfeit
Synonyms: gorge, jade, sate
noun: satiety, satiation
adjective: satiable
verb: satiate

Even an "all you can eat" feast failed to **satiate** his hunger.

35:15

"I have also sent to you all My servants the prophets, rising up early and sending them, saying, 'Turn now everyone from his evil way, <u>amend</u> your doings, and do not go after other gods to serve them; then you will dwell in the land which I have given you and your fathers.' But you have not inclined your ear, nor obeyed Me.

Definition: improve
Synonyms: right, rectify, amend
noun: amender
adjective: amendable
verb: amend

Making **amends** can prevent hurt feelings after an argument.

36:23

And it happened, when Jehudi had read three or four columns, that the king cut it with the scribe's knife and cast it into the fire that was on the <u>hearth</u>, until all the scroll was consumed in the fire that was on the hearth.

Definition: area in front of a fireplace; home
noun: hearth, hearthstone

Families often spend quality time in front of the **hearth**.

46:21

Also her <u>mercenaries</u> are in her midst like fat bulls, For they also are turned back, They have fled away together. They did not stand, For the day of their calamity had come upon them, The time of punishment.

Definition: hired soldier; serving only for money
Synonyms: hacks, drudges, grubs, grubbers, hirelings
noun: mercenary, mercenariness
adjective: mercenary
adverb: mercenarily

The rebels were a ragtag group of political dissidents and **mercenaries**.

51:7

Babylon was a golden cup in the LORD's hand, That made all the earth drunk. The nations drank wine; Therefore the nations are <u>deranged</u>.

Definition: disarranged or upset; make insane
Synonyms: disordered, distraught, disarrayed, disarranged, disorganized, disrupted
noun: derangement
verb: derange

Deranged patients must be kept in straightjackets at all time according to hospital regulations.

LAMENTATIONS

LAMENTATIONS
2:14

Your prophets have seen for you False and <u>deceptive</u> visions; They have not uncovered your iniquity, To bring back your captives, But have envisioned for you false prophecies and delusions.
Definition: act or fact of deceiving; fraud
Synonyms: misleading, beguiling, deceiving, deluding, delusive, delusory, fallacious, false
noun: deception, deceptiveness
adjective: deceptive
adverb: deceptively
Large grizzly bears are **deceptively** quick .

5:3

We have become orphans and <u>waifs</u>, Our mothers are like widows.
Definition: homeless child
noun: waif
The little **waifs** engendered compassion in the social workers.

Random Review - Jeremiah & Lamentations

Match the numbered words with their lettered definitions. Check your answers in the back of the book.

1.	ordained		a.	decreed
2.	lye		b.	reddish orange
3.	dromedary		c.	take the place of
4.	desolate		d.	sarcastic insult
5.	supplant		e.	easily managed
6.	exhorted		f.	speedy one-humped camels
7.	docile		g.	insane
8.	catastrophe		h.	home
9.	vermilion		i.	corrosive alkaline substance
10.	taunt		j.	improve
11.	satiate		k.	urge earnestly
12.	amend		l.	satisfy
13.	hearth		m.	lifeless
14.	mercenaries		n.	disaster
15.	deranged		o.	hired soldiers
16.	deceptive		p.	homeless child
17.	waif		q.	fraud

Try These

Use the complete vocabulary list from the specified book to fill in the missing word for each verse.

Jeremiah

31:14
I will _____ the soul of the priests with abundance, And all my people shall be satisfied with My goodness," says the LORD.

Lamentations

2:14
Your prophets have seen for you False and _____ visions; They have not uncovered your iniquity, To bring back your captives, But have envisioned for you false prophecies and delusions.

EZEKIEL

EZEKIEL
1:7
Their legs were straight, and the soles of their feet were like the soles of calves; feet. They sparkled like the color of <u>burnished</u> bronze.
Definition: polish
Synonyms: lustrous, gleaming, glistening, glossy, polished, sheeny, shining
noun: burnisher
verb: burnish
A ceremonial sword of **burnished** steel was ordered but never delivered.
2:4
"For they are <u>impudent</u> and stubborn children. I am sending you to them, and you shall say to them, "Thus says the LORD GOD."
Definition: lacking proper respect
Synonyms: wise, bold, cheeky, forward, fresh, insolent, nervy, pert, sassy, smart
noun: impudence
adjective: impudent
adverb: impudently
Being **impudent** toward those trying to help is counterproductive.
3:9
"Like <u>adamant</u> stone, harder than flint, I have made your forehead; do not be afraid of them, nor be dismayed at their looks, though they are a rebellious house."
Definition: very hard stone; insistent
Synonyms: inflexible, adamantine, dogged, inexorable, iron, obdurate, relentless, rigid, steadfast, stubborn, unbendable, unbending, uncompromising
noun: adamant
adjective: adamant, adamantine
adverb: adamantly
She **adamantly** refused to violate her ethics.
4:9
"Also take for yourself wheat, barley, beans, lentils, <u>millet</u>, and spelt; put them into one vessel, and make bread of them for yourself. During the number of days that you lie on your side, three hundred and ninety days, you shall eat it.
Definition: cereal and forage grass with small seeds
noun: millet
While camping in the mountain, we cooked our own **millet** for breakfast.
13:10
"Because indeed, because they have seduced My people, saying, "Peace!"

when there is no peace -and one builds a boundary wall, and they plaster it with <u>untempered</u> mortar-
Definition: not strong or tough
Synonyms: softened
adjective: untempered
Untempered swords will break in battle.

14:9

"And if the prophet is induced to speak anything, I the LORD have <u>induced</u> that prophet, and I will stretch out My hand against him and destroy him from among My people Israel.
Definition: persuade; bring about
Synonyms: argued into, brought around, convinced, drew/drawn, drew in/drawn in, prevailed on, prevailed upon procured, prompted, talked into, won over
noun: inducement, inducer, inducibility
adjective: inducible
verb: induce
Peer pressure **induced** him to do what he knew was wrong.

19:11

She had strong branches for scepters of rulers. She towered in stature above the thick branches, And was seen in her height amid the dense <u>foliage</u>.
Definition: plant leaves
Synonyms: leafage, umbrage verdure
noun: foliage
adjective: foliaged
Thick **foliage** slowed our progress through the jungle.

20:49

Then I said, "Ah LORD GOD! They say of me, "Does he not speak <u>parables</u>?"
Definition: simple story illustrating a moral truth
Synonyms: allegories, fables, myths
noun: parable
As children, we learned our morals from **parables**.

21:30

"Return it to its sheath. I will judge you in the place where you were created, In the land of your <u>nativity</u>.
Definition: act or fact of being born or of producing young
noun: birth, birthday, birthplace, birthrate
Many Americans have **nativities** outside of this nation.

23:20

For she lusted for her <u>paramours</u>, Whose flesh is like the flesh of donkeys, the issue of horses.

Definition: illicit lover
Synonyms: lovers, boyfriends, fancy men, men, masters
noun: paramour
She knew that it was risky to be seen in public with her **paramour**.
    23:24
And they shall come against you With chariots, wagons and war-horses, With a <u>horde</u> of people. They shall array against you Buckler, shield, and helmet all around.
Definition: throng or swarm
Synonyms: crowd, crush, drove, multitude, press
noun: horde
Hordes of honeybees escaped from the bee farm.
    27:5
They made all your planks of fir trees from Senir; They took a cedar from Lebanon to make you a <u>mast</u>.
Definition: tall pole supporting sails
noun: mast
adjective: masted
The ship's **mast** snapped during a rough thunderstorm.
    27:19
"Dan and Javan paid for your wares, <u>traversing</u> back and forth. Wrought iron, cassia, and cane were among your merchandise.
Definition: go or extend across or over
Synonyms: perambulating, walking, crossing, traveling
noun: traversal, traverse, traverser
adjective: traversable
verb: traverse
We managed to find a narrower point at which to **traverse** the river.
    27:29
All who handle the oar, The <u>mariners</u>, All the pilots of the sea Will come down from their ships and stand on the shore.
Definition: sailors
Synonyms: seamen
noun: mariner
Mariners once believed that the world was flat.
    29:19
Therefore thus says the LORD GOD: "Surely I will give the land of Egypt to Nebuchadnezzar king of Babylon; he shall take away her wealth, carry off her spoil, and remove her <u>pillage</u>; and that will be the wages for his army.
Definition: take booty
Synonyms: ravage, depredate, desecrate, devastate, devour, waste

noun: pillage, pillager
verb: pillage
Pirates **pillaged** villages along the coastline.
   31:4
The waters made it grow; Underground waters gave it height, With their rivers running around the place where it was planted And sent out <u>rivulets</u> to all the trees of the field.
Definition: small stream
Synonyms: creek, brook, gill, race, runnel, stream
noun: rivulet
Crayfish are abundant in this **rivulet**.
   32:10
"Yes, I will make many peoples astonished at you, and their kings shall be horribly afraid of you when I <u>brandish</u> My sword before them; and they shall tremble every moment, every man for his own life in the day of your fall.'
Definition: wave
Synonyms: show display, disport, exhibit, expose, flash, flaunt, parade, show off, trot out
verb: brandish
A **brandished** gun silenced the crowd.

Random Review - Ezekiel

Match the numbered words with their lettered definitions. Check your answers in the back of the book.

1.	burnished	a.	persuaded
2.	impudent	b.	moral stories
3.	adamant	c.	cereal with small seeds
4.	millet	d.	take booty
5.	untempered	e.	wave
6.	induced	f.	sailors
7.	foliage	g.	small strea
8.	parables	h.	lacking respect
9.	paramours	i.	sail support
10.	horde	j.	not strong
11.	mast	k.	insistent
12.	mariners	l.	swarm
13.	pillage	m.	illicit lovers
14.	rivulets	n.	plant leaves
15.	brandish	o.	polished

Try These

Use the complete vocabulary list from the specified book to fill in the missing word for each verse.

Ezekiel

14:9
"And if the prophet is induced to speak anything, I the LORD have _____ that prophet, and I will stretch out My hand against him and destroy him from among My people Israel.

27:19
"Dan and Javan paid for your wares, _____ back and forth. Wrought iron, cassia, and cane were among your merchandise.

DANIEL

DANIEL

3:27

And the satraps, administrators, governors, and the king's counselors gathered together, and they saw these men on whose bodies the fire had no power; the hair of their head was not <u>singed</u> nor were their garments affected, and the smell of fire was not on them.

Definition: scorch lightly
verb: singe
We escaped from the inferno barely **singed**.

5:20

"But when his heart was lifted up, and his spirit was hardened in pride, he was <u>deposed</u> from his kingly throne, and they took his glory from him.

Definition: removed (a ruler) from office
Synonyms: dethroned, displaced
verb: depose
The Shah of Iran was **deposed** despite support from the U.S.

6:3

Then this Daniel distinguished himself above the governors and satraps, because an excellent spirit was in him; and the king gave thought to setting him over the whole <u>realm</u>.

Definition: kingdom; sphere
Synonyms: confines, extension, extent, purview, reach, scope
noun: realm
The queen determined that she would rule all the **realms** of the earth.

6:26

I make a decree that in every dominion of my kingdom men must tremble and fear before the God of Daniel. For He is the living God, And <u>steadfast</u> forever; His kingdom is the one which shall not be destroyed, And His dominion shall endure to the end.

Definition: faithful or determined
Synonyms: immovable, fixed, immobile, irremovable, unmovable
noun: steadfastness
adjective: steadfastly
verb: steadfast
Our allies have always been **steadfast**.

10:8

Therefore I was left alone when I saw this great vision, and no strength remained in me; for my <u>vigor</u> was turned to frailty in me, and I retained no strength.

Definition: energy or strength; intensity or force
Synonyms: power, might, potency, puissance, sinew, steam, virtue

noun: vigor, vigorousness
adjective: vigorous
adverb: vigorousness
With morale high, we attacked with **vigor**.

HOSEA

HOSEA
    9:6

For indeed they are gone because of destruction. Egypt shall gather them up; Memphis shall bring them. <u>Nettles</u> shall posess their valuables of silver; Thorns shall be in their tents.

Definition: edible plant
noun: nettle
While lost in the wilderness, we survived by eating **nettles**.

JOEL

JOEL
7:6
Before them people <u>writhe</u> in pain; All faces are drained of color.
Definition: move or proceed with twists and turns
Synonyms: agonize, squirm, toss
verb: writhe
Poison ivy sufferers **writhe** with irritation.

AMOS

AMOS
    5:13
Therefore the <u>prudent</u> keep silent at that time,
For it is a evil time.
Definition: shrewd, cautious, thrifty
Synonyms: wise, judicious, sage, sapient, sensible, expedient, advisable, politic, tactical
noun: prudence
adjective: prudential
adverb: prudentially, prudently
A **prudent** person will consider the consequences before acting.
    7:7
Thus He showed me: Behold, the Lord stood on a wall made with a <u>plumb</u> line, with a plumb line in His hand.
Definition: weight on the end of a line to show vertical direction
Synonyms: sound, fathom, perpendicular
noun: plumb
adjective: plumb
verb: plumb
adverb: plumb
A **plumb** line was dropped from the longboat to determine water depth.

OBADIAH

OBADIAH

OBADIAH

1:7

All the men in your <u>confederacy</u> shall force you to the border; The men at peace with you shall deceive you and prevail against you. Those who eat your bread shall lay a trap for you. No one is aware of it.

Definition: league
Synonyms: alliance, coalition, confederation, federation, union
noun: confederacy

The city-states of Greece were organized into a **confederacy.**

1:13

You should not have entered the gate of My people
In the day of their <u>calamity</u>.
Indeed, you should not have gazed on their affliction
In the day of calamity,
Nor laid hands on their substance
In the day of their calamity.

Definition: disaster
Synonyms: disaster, cataclysm, catastrophe, misadventure, tragedy, woes
noun: calamity, calamitousness
adjective: calamitous
adverb: calamitously

Calamitous floods ruined most of this season's crop.

1:15

For the day of the LORD upon all nations is near; As you have done, it shall be done to you; Your <u>reprisal</u> shall return upon your own head.

Definition: act in retaliation
Synonyms: retaliation, avenging, counterblow, requital, retribution, revanche, revenge, vengeance
noun: reprisal

Gang members face constant **reprisals** for their crimes.

JONAH

JONAH

1:11

Then they said to him, "what shall we do to you that the sea may be calm for us?" - for the sea was growing <u>tempestuous</u>

Definition: violent storm
Synonyms: wild, blustering, blustery, dirty, furious, raging, rough, storming, turbulent
noun: tempestuousness
adjective: tempestuous
adverb: tempestuously

We were nearly capsized by the **tempestuous** ocean.

2:3

For you cast me into the deep, Into the heart of the seas, And the foods surrounded me; All Your <u>billows</u> and Your waves passed over me.

Definition: great wave; rolling waves
noun: billow
adjective: billowy
verb: billow

Clouds **billowed** through the sky.

3:9

"Who can tell if God will turn and <u>relent</u>, and turn away from His fierce anger, so that we may not perish?"

Definition: became less severe
Synonyms: abate, die down, die away, ease off, ebb, fall, let up, lull, moderate, slacken, subside, wane
verb: relent

Refusing to **relent**, the coach had his team run up the scores even after the game was won.

Random Review - Daniel, Hosea, Joel, Amos, Obadiah, & Jonah

Match the numbered words with their lettered definitions. Check your answers in the back of the book.

1. realm
2. steadfast
3. vigor
4. writhe
5. plumb
6. confederacy
7. reprisal
8. billows

a. energy
b. retaliation
c. twist and turn
d. league
e. kingdom
f. great waves
g. weight on end of lime
h. determined

Try These

Use the complete vocabulary list from the specified book to fill in the missing word for each verse.

Daniel

3:27
And the _____, administrators, governors, and the king's counselors gathered together, and they saw these men on whose bodies the fire had no power; the hair of their head was snot singed nor were their garments affected, and the smell of fire was not on them.

Joel

7:6
Before them people _____ in pain; All faces are drained of color.

Obadiah

1:15
For the day of the LORD upon all nations is near; As you have done, it shall be done to you; Your _____ shall return upon your own head.

MICAH

MICAH
1:7
All her carved images shall be beaten to pieces,
And all her pay as a harlot shall be burned with fire;
All her idols I will lay <u>desolate</u>,
For she gathered it from the pay of a harlot,
And they shall return to the pay of a harlot."
Definition: lifeless, disconsolate; lay waste
Synonyms: derelict, abandoned, deserted, forsaken, solitary, uncouth
noun: desolaters or desolators, desolation
adverb: desolately
World War II left Europe in a state of **desolation.**
2:4
In that day one shall take up a proverb against you, and lament with a bitter lamentation. and say: "We are utterly destroyed! He has changed the heritage of my people; How He has removed it from me! To a <u>turncoat</u> He has devoured our fields.' "
Definition: traitor
Synonyms: renegade, apostate, defector, rat, recreant, tergiversator, turnabout
noun: turncoat
During a war, **turncoats** can be sentenced to death.
3:7
So shall the seers shall be ashamed, and the diviners <u>abashed</u>; Indeed they shall all cover their lips; For there is no answer from God."
Definition: embarrass
Synonyms: confounded, confused, discomfited, disconcerted, discountenanced, fazed, rattled
noun: abashment
verb: abash
The so called chess master was **abashed** by his surprising defeat.

NAHUM

NAHUM

NAHUM

1:6
Who can stand before His indignation?
And who can <u>endure</u> the fierceness of His anger?
His fury is poured out like fire,
And the rocks are thrown down by Him.
Definition: last; suffer patiently; tolerate
Synonyms: continue, abide, carry through, last, persevere, persist, accept, bear with, pocket, swallow, tolerate, tough out
noun: endurance, enduringness
adjective: endurable
verb: endure
adverb: endurably, enduringly
Superior **endurance** is needed to run a marathon.

2:4
The chariots rage in the streets, they <u>jostle</u> one another in the broad roads;
They seem like torches, they run like lightning.
Definition: push or shove
Synonyms: push, bulldoze, elbow, hustle, press, shoulder, shove
verb: jostle
Everybody was **jostled** during the rush hour bus commute.

HABAKKUK

HABAKKUK

1:10

They scoff at kings. And princes are scorned by them. They deride every stronghold. For they heap up mounds of earth and seize it.

Definition: mock
Synonyms: flout, gibe, gird, jeer, jest, quip at, sneer
noun: scoffer
verb: scoff
I **scoffed** at the possibility of life on Mars.

1:15

They take up all of them with a hook, They catch them in their net, And gather them in their dragnet.

Definition: trawl; planned actions for finding a criminal
noun: dragnet
A police **dragnet** was thrown out to catch the escaped convict.

1:16

Therefore they sacrifice to their net, And burn incense to their dragnet; Because by them their share is sumptuous.

Definition: lavish
Synonyms: luxurious, deluxe, luscious, lush, luxuriant, opulent, palace, palatial, plush, plushy, grand, gorgeous, impresario, lavish, splendid
noun: sumptuousness
adjective: sumptuous
adverb: sumptuously
Their historic mansion was **sumptuously** decorated.

ZECHARIAH

ZECHARIAH

ZECHARIAH
6:3
with the third chariot white horses, and with the fourth chariot <u>dappled</u> horses - strong steeds
Definition: mark with colored spots
Synonyms: variegated, discolored, motley, multicolored, parti-colored
noun: dapple
verb: dapple
This litter of kittens is **dappled** with brown markings.
8:2
"Thus says the LORD of hosts; I am zealous for Zion with great zeal; With great <u>fervor</u> I am zealous for her.
Definition: passion
Synonyms: ardor, enthusiasm, fire, hurrah, zeal
noun: fervor, fervency
adjective: fervent
adverb: fervently
In a **fervent** belief that God would protect her, she leapt from a 10th story window.
9:9
"Rejoice greatly, O daughter of Zion! Shout, O daughter of Jerusalem! Behold, Your King is coming to you; He is just and having salvation. Lowly and riding on a donkey, A colt, the <u>foal</u> of a donkey .
Definition: young horse
noun: foal
verb: foal
Due to the unusually frigid temperature, the **foals** spent most of their time in the stable.
12:10
And I will pour on the house of David and on the inhabitants of Jerusalem the spirit of grace and <u>supplication</u>; then they will look on Me whom they have pierced; they will mourn for them as one mourns for his only son, and grieve for Him as one grieves for a firstborn.
Definition: pray to God; ask earnestly and humbly
Synonyms: prayer, appeal, application, entreaty, imprecation, petition, plea, suit
noun: supplicant, supplication
verb: supplicate
Children assume a position of **supplication** when asking their parents for money.

14:2
For I will gather all nations to battle against Jerusalem: The city shall be taken, the houses <u>rifled</u>, And the women ravished. Half of the city shall go into captivity, But the remnant of the people shall not be cut off from the city.
Definition: ransack especially in order to steal
Synonyms: robbed, knocked over, looted, plundered, relieved, stuck up
noun: rifle
verb: rifle
A broken padlock was an alert that someone had **rifled** through her locker.

MALACHI

MALACHI
1:7
"You offer defiled food on My altar. But you say, "In what way have we defiled You?" By saying, "The table of the LORD is contemptible."
Definition: feeling of scorn; state of being despised; disobedience to a court or legislature
Synonyms: despicable, mean, pitiable, pitiful, scummy, scurvy, shabby, sorry
noun: contempt, contemptibleness
adjective: contemptible
adverb: contemptibly
His family's great wealth caused him to think of the poor as **contemptible**.
1:13
You also say, "Oh, what a weariness!" And you sneer at it," Says the LORD of hosts, "And you bring the stolen, the lame, and the sick; Thus you bring an offering! Should I accept this from your hand?" Says the LORD.
Definition: smile scornfully
Synonyms: leer, scoff, flout, gibe, gird, jeer, jest, quip
noun: sneer, sneerer
verb: sneer
The **sneering** faces of the winning team made their loss all the more painful.
2:10
Have we not all one Father? Has not one God created us? Why do we deal treacherously with one another by profaning the covenant of the fathers?
Definition: treat with irreverence; not concerned with religion; serving to debase what is holy
Synonyms: impious, irreverent, ungodly, unholy, sacrilegious, blasphemous
noun: profaneness, profanity, profanation
adverb: profanely
An intruder burst into the morning service and **profaned** the church.
2:17
You have wearied the LORD with your words; yet you say, "In what way have we wearied Him?" In that you say, "Everyone who does evil is good in the sight of the LORD.
Definition: worn out in strength, freshness, or patience
Synonyms: tired, fatigued, jaded, weary, word, worn down
noun: weariness
adjective: weariful, wearliess
verb: wearied
adverb: wearifully, wearilessly
Running in the 400 meter race leaves us **weary**.

Random Review - Micah, Nahum, Habbakuk, Zechariah, & Malachi

Match the numbered words with their lettered definitions. Check your answers in the back of the book.

1. turncoat
2. abashed
3. jostle
4. dragnet
5. sumptuous
6. dappled
7. fervor
8. foal
9. rifled
10. contemptible

a. plan for finding criminals
b. marked with colored spots
c. ransack to steal
d. embarrassed
e. scorned
f. push or shove
g. young horse
h. traitor
i. passion
j. lavish

Try These

Use the complete vocabulary list from the specified book to fill in the missing word for each verse.

Micah

3:7
So shall the seers be ashamed, and the diviners _____; Indeed they shall all cover their lips; For there is no answer from God."

Zechariah

14:2
For I will gather all nations to battle against Jerusalem: The city shall be taken, the houses _____, And the women ravished. Half of the city shall go into captivity, But the remnant of the people shall not be cut off from the city.

MATTHEW

MATTHEW
3:12
"His <u>winnowing</u> fan is in His hand, and He will thoroughly purge His threshing floor, and gather His wheat into the barn; but He will burn up the chaff with unquenchable fire.
Definition: remove (as chaff from grain) by a current of air; get rid of something unwanted or separate something
Synonyms: blow, fan, ruffle, thin, wind
noun: winnower
verb: winnow
The bar exam is used to **winnow** out qualified lawyers from the unprepared.

5:5
Blessed are the <u>meek</u>, For they shall inherit the earth.
Definition: mild-mannered; weak
Synonyms: humble, lowly, modest, unassuming
noun: meekness
adjective: meek
verb: meekly
Being **meek** is not compatible with being a lawyer.

6:24
"No one can serve two masters; for either he will hate the one and love the other, or else he will be loyal to the one and despise the other. You cannot serve God and <u>mammon</u>.
Definition: material wealth especially when seen as having a debasing influence
noun: mammon
Members of a commune abandoned dreams of **mammon** so that they could pursue a more natural course of life.

7:15
"Beware of false prophets, who come to you in sheep's clothing, but inwardly they are <u>ravenous</u> wolves.
Definition: very hungry
Synonyms: voracious, gluttonous, rapacious, ravening
noun: ravenousness
adjective: ravenous
adverb: ravenously
After **gorging** himself on Thanksgiving dinner, he found that he was not quite as **ravenous** as he had been that morning.

8:5
Now when Jesus had entered Capernaum, a <u>centurion</u> came to Him, pleading with Him.

Definition: Roman military officer
noun: centurion
Centurions were used to quell public dissent in the Roman provinces.
    17:2
and was <u>transfigured</u> before them. His face shone like the sun, and His clothes became as white as the light .
Definition: change the form or appearance
Synonyms: transformed, changed, commuted, converted, metamorphosed, mutated, transferred, translated, transmuted
noun: transfiguration
verb: transfigure
After the final day of track events, the stadium was quickly **transfigured** for the music concert.
    23:5
"But all their works they do to be seen by men. They make their <u>phylacteries</u> broad and enlarge the borders of their garments.
Definition: small square leather box containing slips inscribed with scriptural passages
Synonyms: charms, amulets, fetishes, mascots, talismans
noun: phylactery
Even today some groups consider **phylacteries** to have some mystical power.
    23:15
"Woe to you, scribes and Pharisees, hypocrites! For you travel land and sea to make one <u>proselyte</u> and when he is won, you make him twice as much a son of hell as yourself.
Definition: new convert
noun: proselyte, proselytizer
verb: proselyte, proselytize
With great flair, the fiery preacher **proselytized** the unconverted.
    26:7
a woman came to Him having an <u>alabaster</u> flask of very costly fragrant oil, and she poured it on His head as He sat at the table.
Definition: white or translucent mineral
noun: alabaster
The skin of an albino resembles the color of **alabaster**.
    26:28
"For this is My blood of the new covenant, which is shed for many for <u>remission</u> of sins.
Definition: act of forgiving; period of relief from or easing of symptoms of a disease
noun: remission
Chemotherapy treatments forced her cancer into **remission**.

Random Review - Matthew

Match the numbered words with their lettered definitions. Check your answers in the back of the book.

1. winnowing
2. meek
3. mammon
4. ravenous
5. centurion
6. transfigured
7. phylacteries
8. proselyte
9. alabaster
10. remission

a. Roman military officer
b. new convert
c. small square boxes
d. mild-mannered
e. period of relief
f. material wealth
g. white material
h. remove with air
i. change form
j. very hungry

Try These

Use the complete vocabulary list from the specified book to fill in the missing word for each verse.

Matthew

3:12
"His _____ fan is in His hand, and He will thoroughly purge His threshing floor, and gather His wheat into the barn; but He will burn up the chaff with unquenchable fire.

7:15
"Beware of false prophets, who come to you in sheep's clothing, but inwardly they are _____ wolves.

26:28
"For this My blood of the new covenant, which is shed for many for _____ _____ of sins.

MARK

MARK

5:7

And he cried out with a loud voice and said, "What have I to do with You, Jesus, Son of the Most High God? I implore You by God that You do not torment me.

Definition: entreat
Synonyms: beg, appeal, beseech, brace, adjure, crave, importune, invoice, plead, pray, supplicate
verb: implore
adverb: imploringly

Obviously defeated, the captain **implored** the enemy for mercy for his crew.

10:5

And Jesus answered and said to them, "Because of the hardness of your heart he wrote you this precept.

Definition: rule of action or conduct
Synonyms: law, assize, canon, decree, edict, institute, ordinance, prescript, regulation, rule, statue
noun: precept
adjective: preceptize

Violating the **precepts** of a foreign country may do lasting harm to diplomatic relations.

LUKE

LUKE
11:41
But rather give <u>alms</u> of such things as you have; indeed all things are clean to you."
Definition: charitable gift
Synonyms: donation, benefaction, benefice, charity, contribution, offering
noun: alm
It is appropriate to present alms to the poor during the holidays.

14:2
And behold, there was a certain man before Him who had <u>dropsy</u>.
Definition: abnormal accumulation of serous fluid in the body
noun: dropsy
adjective: dropsical
Perhaps **dropsy** is the cause of your light-headedness.

15:13
"And not many days after, the younger son gathered all together, journeyed to a far country, and there wasted his possessions with <u>prodigal</u> living.
Definition: recklessly, extravagant or wasteful
Synonyms: profuse, exuberant, lavish, lush, luxuriant, opulent, riotous
noun: prodigal, prodigality
adjective: prodigal
adverb: prodigally
A **prodigal** lifestyle quickly reduced him from a playboy to a pauper.

19:43
For the days will come upon you when your enemies will build an <u>embankment</u> around you, surround you and close you in on every side.
Definition: protective barrier of earth
noun: embankment
Though some people had doubted the necessity of their construction, the city's **embankments** held against an onslaught of enemy forces.

21:34
"But take heed to yourselves, lest your hearts be weighed down with <u>carousing</u>, drunkenness, and cares of this life, and that Day will come on you unexpectedly.
Definition: drink and be boisterous
Synonyms: reveling, revelling, frolicking, rioting, roistering, wassailing
noun: carouse, carouser
verb: carouse

She had plenty of friends while **carousing** but found herself alone when her money ran out.
23:7
'And as soon as he knew that He belonged to Herod's <u>jurisdiction</u>, he sent Him to Herod, who was also in Jerusalem at that time.
Definition: right or authority to interpret and apply the law
Synonyms: power, authority, control, domination, masterly
noun: jurisdiction
adjective: jurisdictional
We're moving to a **jurisdiction** that assesses a lower tax.

JOHN

JOHN
17:12
"While I was with them in the world, I kept them in Your name. Those whom You gave Me I have kept; and none of them is lost except the son of <u>purgatory</u>, that the scripture may be fulfilled.
Definition: eternal damnation; hell
Synonyms: abyss, blazes, inferno, Pandemonium, pit
noun: purgatory
adjective: purgatorial
Make your peace with God and man before you go to **purgatory**.
18:14
Now it was Caiaphas who gave counsel to the Jews that it was <u>expedient</u> that one man should die for the people.
Definition: convenient or advantageous rather than right or just
Synonyms: advisable, politic, prudent, tactical, wise
noun: expedient
adjective: expedient
adverb: expediently
Carelessness simply for the sake of **expediency** will catch up to you eventually.

Random Review - Mark, Luke, & John

Match the numbered words with their lettered definitions. Check your answers in the back of the book.

1. implore
2. alms
3. dropsy
4. prodigal
5. embankment
6. carousing
7. jurisdiction
8. perdition
9. expedient

a. reckless
b. convenient
c. protective barrier
d. right to interpret law
e. charitable gift
f. hell
g. abnormal accumulation of fluid
h. beg
i. boisterous drinking

Try These

Use the complete vocabulary list from the specified book to fill in the missing word for each verse.

Luke

15:13
"And not many days after, the younger son gathered all together, journeyed to a far country, and there wasted his possessions with _____ living.

21:34
"But take heed to yourselves, lest your hearts be weighed down with _____, drunkenness, and cares of this life, and that Day will come on you unexpectedly.

John

17:12
"While I was with them in the world, I kept them in Your name. Those whom You gave Me I have kept; and none of them is lost except the son of _____, that the scripture may be fulfilled.

ACTS

ACTS
7:8
"Then he gave him the covenant of circumcision; and so Abraham begot Isaac and circumcised him on the eighth day; and Isaac begot Jacob, and Jacob begot the twelve <u>patriarchs</u>.
Definition: man revered as father or founder; venerable old man
Synonyms: father, architect, author, creator, generator, inventor, maker, originator, sire
noun: patriarch, patriarchate, patriarchy
adjective: patriarchal
Being unemployed made him feel as if his role as **patriarch** had been diminished.

8:3
As for Saul, he made <u>havoc</u> of the church, entering every house, and dragging off men and women, committing them to prison.
Definition: wide destruction or great confusion
Synonyms: ruin, destruction, devastation, loss, ruination
noun: havoc
A single drunken driver wreaked **havoc** on a crowded sidewalk.

13:7
who was with the <u>proconsul</u>, Sergius Paulus, an intelligent man. This man called for Barnabas and Saul and sought to hear the word of God.
Definition: governor of an ancient Roman province or modern colony or possession
noun: proconsul, proconsulate
adjective: proconsular
The **proconsul** was unswayed by the thief's protestation of innocence and allowed the sentence to be carried out.

19:13
Then some of the <u>itinerant</u> Jewish exorcists took it upon themselves to call the name of the LORD Jesus over those who had evil spirits, saying "We adjure you by the Jesus whom Paul preaches."
Definition: traveling from place to place
Synonyms: ambulant, nomadic, per ambulatory, peripatetic, roving, vagabond, vagrant, wandering
noun: itinerant
adjective: itinerant
adverb: itinerantly
The children of **itinerant** laborers often have difficulty keeping permanent friendships.

21:20
And when they heard it, they glorified the LORD. And they said to him, "You see, brother, how many <u>myriads</u> of Jews who have believed, and they are all zealous for the law;

Definition: indefinitely large number
noun: myriad
adjective: myriad
Myriad aquatic lifeforms inhabit the depths of the world's oceans and seas.

24:22
But when Felix heard these things, having more accurate knowledge of the Way, he <u>adjourned</u> the proceedings and said, "When Lysias the commander comes down, I will make a decision on your case."

Definition: end a meeting
Synonyms: deferred, delayed, held off, held over, held up, intermitted, laid over, postponed, prorogued, put off, put over, remitted, shelved, stood over, stayed, suspended, waived
noun: adjournment
verb: adjourn
Congress **adjourns** its sessions with a banging of the gavel.

26:14
"And when we all had fallen to the ground, I heard a voice speaking to me and saying in the Hebrew language, "Saul, Saul, why are your persecuting Me? It is hard for you to kick against the <u>goads</u>."

Definition: something that urges
Synonyms: stimuli, catalysts, impetuses, impulses, incentives, incitations, incitements, instigations, motivations, propellants, pushes, spurs, stimulants
noun: goad
verb: goad
She nonchalantly refused to steal from the convenience store despite her friends attempts to **goad** her into doing it.

27:30
And as the sailors were seeking to escape from the ship, when they had let down the <u>skiff</u> into the sea, under pretense of putting out anchors from the prow.

Definition: small open boat
noun: skiff
Our **skiff** was nearly capsized when a thunderstorm suddenly appeared over the lake.

27:40
And they let go the anchors and left them in the sea, meanwhile loosing the

rudder ropes; and they <u>hoisted</u> the mainsail to the wind and made for shore.
Definition: lift, raise, or a device that lifts
Synonyms: elevated, raised, reared, uplifted, upraised
noun: hoist
verb: hoist
A powerful lift was required to **hoist** the sections of the downed airplane from the river.

ROMANS

ROMANS

1:21
because, although they knew God, they did not glorify Him as God, nor were they thankful, but became <u>futile</u> in their thoughts, and were foolish hearts were darkened.
Definition: useless or vain
Synonyms: abortive, bootless, fruitless, ineffective, ineffectual, unavailable, unavailing, unproductive, useless, vain
noun: futileness, futility
adjective: futile
adverb: futilely
Refusing to accept that his own lack of study was the reason for the poor exam score, the student **futilely** tried to get his professor to change the grade.

3:25
whom God set forth to be a <u>propitiation</u> by His blood, through faith, to demonstrate His righteousness, because in His forbearance God has passed over the sins that were previously committed,
Definition: gain or regain the favor of
noun: propitiation, propitiator
adjective: propitiatory
verb: propitiate
The children **propitiated** the situation by agreeing to work off their debt.

11:8
Just as it is written:
"God has given them a spirit of <u>stupor</u>,
Eyes that they should not see
And ears that they should not hear,
To this very day."
Definition: state of being conscious but not aware or sensible
Synonyms: lethargy, coma, dullness, languor, lassitude, sleep, slumber, torpidity, torpor
noun: stupor
adjective: stuporous
Too much liquor left him in a drunken **stupor**.

15:1
We then who are strong ought to bear with the <u>scruples</u> of the weak, and not to please ourselves.
Definition: reluctance due to ethical considerations
Synonyms: qualms, compunctions, consciences, demurs
noun: scruple, scrupulousness

adjective: scrupulous
verb: scruple
adverb: scrupulously
She always prides herself on her ability to make **scrupulous** decisions even when the majority disagrees.

Random Review - Acts & Romans

Match the numbered words with their lettered definitions. Check your answers in the back of the book.

1.	patriarchs	a.	large numbers
2.	havoc	b.	urges
3.	proconsul	c.	lifted
4.	itinerant	d.	traveling
5.	myriads	e.	act of gaining favor
6.	adjourned	f.	ended a meeting
7.	goads	g.	conscious but unaware state
8.	skiff	h.	fathers
9.	hoisted	i.	useless
10.	futile	j.	destruction or confusion
11.	propitiation	k.	small, open boat
12.	stupor	l.	ethical considerations
13.	scruples	m.	governor of Roman province

Try These

Use the complete vocabulary list from the specified book to fill in the missing word for each verse.

Acts

21:20
And when they heard it, they glorified the LORD. And they said to him, "You see, brother, how many _____ of Jews who have believed, and they are all zealous for the law;

Romans

11:8
Just as it is written:
"God has given them a spirit of _____ ,
Eyes that they should not see
And ears that they should not hear,
To this very day."

CORINTHIANS I

CORINTHIANS I
5:9

I wrote to you in my <u>epistle</u> not to keep company with sexually immoral people.
Definition: letter
Synonyms: missive, note
noun: epistle, epistler
The Pope regularly sends **epistles** to Catholic churches around the world.
12:25

that there should be no <u>schism</u> in the body, but that the members should have the same care for one another.
Definition: split
Synonyms: breach, break, fissure, fracture, rent, rift, rupture, heresy, dissent, dissidence, heterodoxy, misbelief, nonconformity, unorthodoxy, cleft, chasm
noun: schism, schismatic
adjective: schismatic
A **schism** led to the split of the Protestant church from the Roman Catholic one.
14:4

He who speaks in a tongue, <u>edifies</u> himself, but he who prophesies edifies the church.
Definition: instruct or inform
Synonyms: illuminate, enlighten, illumine, improve, irradiate, uplift
noun: edification
verb: edify
I had to listen to a police officer **edify** me about state speed limits.

CORINTHIANS II

CORINTHIANS II

2:17

For we are not, as many, <u>peddling</u> the word of God; but as of sincerity, but as from God, we speak in the sight of God in Christ.

Definition: offer for sale
Synonyms: hawking, mongering, vending
noun: peddler
verb: peddle

Local law prohibits **peddling** on sidewalks.

9:1

Now concerning the ministering to the saints, it is <u>superfluous</u> for me to write to you;

Definition: more than necessary
Synonyms: excess, spare, supernumerary, surplus
noun: superfluidity, superfluousness
adjective: superfluous
adverb: superfluously

This **superfluous** food should be donated to a homeless shelter rather than simply throwing it away.

11:5

For I consider that I am not at all inferior to the most <u>eminent</u> apostles.

Definition: prominent
Synonyms: famous, celebrated, distinguished, famed, great, illustrious, notable, prestigious, prominent, redoubtable, renowned
noun: eminence
adjective: eminent
adverb: eminently

Traditionally, numerous heads of state are dubbed "Your **Eminence**."

12:21

and lest, when I come again, my God will humble me among you, and I shall mourn for many who have sinned before and have not repented of the uncleanness, fornication, and <u>licentiousness</u> which they have practiced.

Definition: disregarding sexual restraints
Synonyms: dissoluteness, unprincipledness, lewdness, lustfulness, salaciousness
noun: licentiousness
adjective: licentious
adverb: licentiously

Most senior citizens think that the present generation is too **licentious.**

Random Review - Corinthians I & II

Match the numbered words with their lettered definitions. Check your answers in the back of the book.

1. epistle
2. schism
3. superfluous
4. peddling
5. prominent

a. offering for sale
b. famous
c. letter
d. more than necessary
e. split

Try These

Use the complete vocabulary list from the specified book to fill in the missing word for each verse.

Corinthians I

12:25
that there should be no _____ in the body, but that the members should have the same care for one another.

Corinthians II

2:17
For we are not, as many, _____ the word of God; but as of sincerity, but as from God, we speak in the sight of God in Christ.

9:1
Now concerning the ministering to the saints, it is _____ for me to write to you;

GALATIANS

GALATIANS

GALATIANS
    2:4

But this occurred because of false brethren secretly brought in (who came in stealth to spy out our liberty which we have in Jesus Christ, that they might bring us into bondage).
Definition: secretly
noun: stealth, stealthiness
adjective: stealth
adverb: stealthily
Figuring that **stealth** would win more battles than sheer might, the general ordered his troops to attack under cover of darkness.

EPHESIANS

EPHESIANS
>4:31

Let all bitterness, wrath, anger, <u>clamor</u> and evil speaking be put away from you, with all malice.
Definition: uproar; protest
Synonyms: commotion, convulsion, ferment, outcry, tumult, upheaval, upturn
noun: clamor, clamorousness
adjective: clamorous
verb: clamor
adverb: clamorously
The gathered neighborhood activists **clamored** against the proposed stadium.
>6:11

Put on the whole armor of God, that you may be able to stand against the <u>wiles</u> of the devil.
Definition: trick to snare or deceive
Synonyms: tricks, artifices, devices, feints, gambits, gimmicks, jigs, maneuvers, plays, ploys, ruses, shenanigans, sleights, stratagems
noun: wile
verb: wile
Using the promise of fame and fortune as a **wile**, recording executives convince aspiring musicians to sign contracts that they have not read.
>6:12

For we do not wrestle against flesh and blood, but against <u>principalities</u>, against powers, against the rulers of the darkness of this age, against the spiritual hosts of wickedness in the heavenly places.
Definition: territory of a prince
noun: principality
To cement her rule over the entire nation, the queen divided it into five **principalities** and appointed her children as rulers.

PHILIPPIANS

PHILIPPIANS

1:9
And this I pray, that your love may <u>abound</u> still more and more in knowledge and all discernment.
Definition: be plentiful
Synonyms: teem, flow, swarm
verb: abound
Since I ceased feeling sorry for myself, good luck has **abounded**.

1:28
and not anyway terrified by your <u>adversaries,</u> which is to them a proof of perdition, but to you of salvation, and that from God.
Definition: enemy or rival
Synonyms: opponents, antagonists, antis, cons, matches
noun: adversary
adjective: adversarial
The soccer defeated its **adversaries** and won the championship.

4:12
I know how to be <u>abased</u>, and I know how to abound. Everywhere and in all things I have learned to be both full and hungry, both to abound and to suffer need.
Definition: lower in dignity
Synonyms: humbled, cast down, debased, degraded, demeaned, humiliated, lowered, sank or sunk
noun: abasement
verb: abase
Losing the battle to a smaller but more skilled force left the soldiers feeling unworthy and **abased**.

COLOSSIANS

COLOSSIANS

COLOSSIANS
1:18
And He is the head of the body, the church, who is the beginning, the first-born from the dead, that in all things He may have the <u>preeminence</u>.
Definition: having highest rank
Synonyms: supremacy, ascendency, ascendant, dominance, dominion, preponderance, eminence, distinction, illustriousness, kudos, prestige, prominence, renown
noun: preeminence
adjective: preeminent
adverb: preeminently
The Supreme Court holds **preeminence** over all state and federal courts.
1:20
and by Him to <u>reconcile</u> all things to Himself, by Him, whether things on earth or things in heaven, having made peace through the blood of cross.
Definition: cause to be friendly again; adjust or settle; bring to acceptance
Synonyms: harmonize, accommodate, attune, conform
noun: reconcilability, reconcilement, reconciler, reconciliation
adjective: reconcilable
verb: reconcile
In the decades following World War II, Germany was **reconciled** with Europe.

Random Review - Galatians, Ephesians, Phillipians, & Colossians

Match the numbered words with their lettered definitions. Check your answers in the back of the book.

1. stealth
2. clamor
3. wiles
4. principalities
5. abased
6. preeminence

a. uproar
b. territories
c. lowered in dignity
d. tricks
e. highest rank
f. secretly

Try These

Use the complete vocabulary list from the specified book to fill in the missing word for each verse.

Galatians

2:4
But this occurred because of false brethren secretly brought in (who came in _____ to spy out our liberty which we have in Jesus Christ, that they might bring us into bondage).

Ephesians

6:11
Put on the whole armor of God, that you may be able to stand against the _____ of the devil.

4:12
I know how to be _____ , and I know how to abound. Everywhere and in all things I have learned to be both full and hungary, both to abound and to suffer need.

TIMOTHY I

TIMOTHY I

TIMOTHY I

1:9

knowing this: that the law is not made for a righteous person, but for the lawless and <u>insubordinate</u>, for the ungodly and for sinners, for the unholy and profane, for murderers of fathers and murderers of mothers, for manslayers.

Definition: not obeying
Synonyms: contumacious, factious, insurgent, rebellious, seditious
noun: insubordination
adjective: insubordinate
adverb: insubordinately
Insubordination will land you in the brig.

6:5

useless wranglings of men of corrupt minds and <u>destitute</u> of the truth, who suppose that godliness is a means of gain. From such withdraw yourself.

Definition: lacking something; very poor
Synonyms: poor, devoid, empty, impecunious, impoverished, indigent, low, necessitous, needy, penurious, stony, strapped, unprospered
noun: destitution
adjective: destitute
The stock market crash of 1929 left many families **destitute**.

TIMOTHY II

TIMOTHY II

3:6

For of this sort are those who creep into households and make captives of <u>gullible</u> women loaded down with sins, led away by various lusts,

Definition: make a dupe of
Synonyms: easy, naive, susceptible
noun: gull, gullibility
adjective: gullible
verb: gull
adverb: gullibly

His **gullibility**, while refreshing, led to his constantly being taken advantage of.

4:2

Preach the word! Be ready in season and out of season. Convince, <u>rebuke</u>, exhort, with all longsuffering and teaching.

Definition: reprimand sharply
Synonyms: reprove, admonish, call down, chide, reprimand, reproach
noun: rebuke
verb: rebuke

After the facts of her speech were proven wrong, the politician was publicly **rebuked**.

TITUS

TITUS
1:6

if a man is blameless, the husband of one's wife, having faithful children not accused of <u>dissipation</u> or insubordination.
Definition: break up and drive off; squander; drink to excess
Synonyms: entertainment, amusement, distraction, diversion, divertissement, recreation
noun: dissipation, dissipator
verb: dissipate
Hordes of Huns were **dissipated** by Roman armies.

2:9

But avoid foolish disputes, genealogies, <u>contentions</u> and strivings about the law; for they are unprofitable and useless.
Definition: state of contending
Synonyms: controversy, discord, opposition, quarrel, strife
noun: contentions, contentiousness, contender
adjective: contentious
verb: contend
adverb: contentiously
Democrats and Republicans often **contend** over meaningless issues.

2:10

not <u>pilfering</u>, but showing all goods <u>fidelity</u>, that they may adorn the doctrine of God our savior in all things.
Definition: steal in small quantities at a time
Synonyms: abstracting, annexing, appropriating, collaring, filching, hooking, lifting, nabbing, nipping, pillaging, pinching, pocketing, purloining, swiping, thieving
noun: pilferage, pilferer
verb: pilfer
The manager of a doughnut shop noticed that his inventory was always less than what it should have been; he suspected a **pilferer**.
Definition: quality or state of being faithful; quantity of reproduction
Synonyms: allegiance, ardor, devotion, faithfulness, fealty, loyalty, piety
noun: fidelity
Fidelity is an essential component of a successful marriage.

JAMES

JAMES
   3:9
With it we bless our God and Father, and with it we curse men, who have been made in the similitude of God.
Definition: likeness
Synonyms: affinity, resemblance, semblance, similarity
noun: similitude
Though they were twins, the **similitude** between them was uncanny.

PETER II

PETER II
2:11

whereas angels, who are greater in power,, and might, do not bring a <u>reviling</u> accusation against them before the Lord.

Definition: abuse verbally
Synonyms: berate, rebuke, vilify, vituperate
noun: revilement, reviler
verb: revile
The fiery preacher **reviled** the sinners in his congregation.

2:14

having eyes full of adultery and that cannot cease from sin, <u>beguiling</u> unstable souls. They have 'a heart trained in covetous practices, and are accursed children.

Definition: deceive, amuse
Synonyms: cheat, defraud, delude, dupe, entrap, mislead, outwit, trick
noun: beguilement, beguiler
verb: beguile
adverb: beguilingly
A crafty salesman **beguiled** us out of $5,000.

Random Review - Timothy I & II, Titus, James, & Peter II

Match the numbered words with their lettered definitions. Check your answers in the back of the book.

1. insubordinate
2. destitute
3. gullible
4. pilfering
5. similitude

a. very poor
b. stealing small quantities
c. naive
d. not obeying
e. likeness

Try These

Use the complete vocabulary list from the specified book to fill in the missing word for each verse.

Timothy I

6:5
useless wranglings of men of corrupt minds and ———— of the truth, who suppose that godliness is a means of gain. From such withdraw yourself.

Titus

2:10
not ———————— , but showing all goods fidelity, that they may adorn the doctrine of God our savior in all things.

James

3:9
With it we bless our God and Father, and with it we curse men, who have been made in the ———————— of God.

Rooted In The Word

(Roots and Affixes)

ROOTED IN THE WORD

Vocabulary is the root of all knowledge! Here is a list of some frequently used roots and the "bible-based" SAT, GRE, and advanced vocabulary words that are desired from them! Now that you have attempted to become "grounded in the word" your vocabulary can be "rooted in the word."

a (without)
- abased
- amend
- amiss
- annihilate
- annul

ab/abs (off, away, from, apart, down)
- abashed
- abhorrent
- abomination
- ascending

ad/al (to, toward, near)
- adamant
- adjoin
- adjourned
- admonished
- allotted
- alloy
- allure

am/em (love)
- paramour

amb (go walk)
- ambush

apo (away)
- apportion

be (to be, have a certain quality)
- befall
- bereaved
- besiege
- betrothed
- bewailed

cap/cip/cept (take, get)
- principalities
- receptacles

cast/chast (cut)
- chastening

ced/ceed/cess (go, yield, stop)
- intercessor
- recesses

chron (time)
- chronicles

circu (around, on all sides)
- circumspect

cit (set in motion)
- incited

clam/claim (shout, cry out)
- clamor

cla/clo/clu (shut, close)
- cloven
- disclose
- seclusion

co/col/com/con/cor (with, together)
- commemorate
- compelled
- compensate
- complacency
- compulsory
- conciliation
- concourses
- confederacy
- confer
- confiscation
- confounded
- congealed
- conspire
- constituency
- consummation
- contemptible
- contingent
- convex
- convocation
- reconcile

ROOTED IN THE WORD

cur, cour (running a course)
concourse
currency
discourse

de (away, off, down, reverse)
debases
deferred
degenerate
delegate
delusions
denounce
deplete
deploy
deposed
deranged
derision
descending

di/dia (apart, though)
diadem

dis/dif (away from, apart, reversal, not)
discerning
disclose
discourse
disdained
dismayed
disposed
distraught

doc (teach)
docile

epi (upon)
epistle

ex/e/ef (out, out of, from, former, completely)
edict
eloquent
emasculated
emitted
estranged
exacted
exhorted
expedient
expedition
extolled
extorted

fer (bring, carry, bear)
confer
deferred
pilfering

ferv (bubble, boil, burn)
fervor

flict (strike)
afflict

gen (birth, creation, kind, race)
contingents
degenerate
genealogy

gn/gno/ogn (know)
indignant
prognosticators

gress/grad (step)
transgression

ROOTED IN THE WORD

In/im/en/em (in, into)
eminent
encampment
endearment
endowment
enmity
entrails
envoys
implore
incite
intoxicating
preeminence

in/im (not, without)
indignant
iniquity
insubordinate

join/junct (meet, join)
adjoin

lev (lift, light, rise)
leviathan
levy

loc/log/loqu (word, speech)
eloquent

mal/male (bad, evil, ill, wrong)
malady
malicious

man (hand)
manifold

min (protect, hang over)
abomination
eminent
preeminence

mon/monit (warn)
admonished

nam/nom/nown/noun (name)
Deuteronomy

ob/oc/of/op (toward, to against, completely, over)
obscure
obstinate

para (next to, beside)
parables
paramours
parapet

pen/pun (pay, compensate)
penitent

per (completely, wrong)
perdition
perpetual

phil (love)
philistine

plac (please)
complacency

pon, pos, pound (put, place)
deposed
disposed
posterity

port (to carry)
apportioned
portico

ROOTED IN THE WORD

pro (much, for, a lot)
prominent
proselyte
prostrate

rid/ris (laugh)
derision

sanct/sacr/secr (sacred)
sanctified

sci (known)
discern

sol (loosen, free)
insolence

sta (stand, be in place)
constituency
destitute
obstinate
posterity
restitution
stature
steadfast

se (apart)
seclusion
sedition
sepulcher

scribe/scrip (write)
ascribe
scribe

tain/ten/tent/tin (hold)
contingents
retinue
sustenance

trans (across)
transfigured
transgression
transversing

us/ut (use)
futility

ver (truth)
verify

vers/vert (turn)
adversities
subvert
transversing

vi (life)
vigor

voc/vok (call)
convocation

Answers to Random Review

Answers to Random Review

Genesis
1. c
2. j
3. g
4. a
5. h
6. b
7. e
8. d
9. i
10. f

Exodus
1. e
2. h
3. a
4. g
5. c
6. j
7. i
8. b
9. f
10. d

Leviticus
1. e
2. j
3. g
4. a
5. c
6. b
7. d
8. h
9. f
10. i

Numbers
1. f
2. c
3. j
4. h
5. a
6. b
7. e
8. i
9. g
10. d

Deuteronomy
1. d
2. j
3. a
4. g
5. b
6. i
7. c
8. e
9. h
10. f

Joshua / Judges
1. j
2. a
3. e
4. h
5. b
6. i
7. c
8. d
9. f
10. g

Samuel I & II
1. h
2. o
3. a
4. k
5. e
6. m
7. c
8. b
9. g
10. d
11. f
12. n
13. i
14. j
15. l

Kings I & II
1. k
2. g
3. i
4. a
5. o
6. d
7. m
8. b
9. f
10. c
11. n
12. e
13. h
14. l
15. j

Chronicles I & II
1. g
2. b
3. h
4. e
5. a
6. d
7. c
8. f

Ezra / Nehemiah / Esther
1. a
2. j
3. e
4. h
5. b
6. i
7. c
8. d
9. g
10. f
11. m
12. l
13. k

323

Answers to Random Review

	Job		Ecclesiastes / Song of Solomon		Jeremiah / Lamentations
1.	g	1.	j	1.	a
2.	b	2.	g	2.	j
3.	j	3.	d	3.	f
4.	o	4.	a	4.	m
5.	c	5.	i	5.	c
6.	m	6.	b	6.	k
7.	k	7.	h	7.	e
8.	g	8.	f	8.	n
9.	n	9.	e	9.	b
10.	d	10.	c	10.	d
11.	h			11.	l
12.	e		**Isaiah**	12.	j
13.	i	1.	k	13.	h
14.	l	2.	a	14.	o
15.	f	3.	h	15.	g
		4.	o	16.	q
	Psalms	5.	m	17.	p
1.	g	6.	b		
2.	j	7.	e		**Ezekiel**
3.	n	8.	n	1.	o
4.	d	9.	d	2.	h
5.	l	10.	f	3.	k
6.	o	11.	l	4.	c
7.	a	12.	j	5.	j
8.	f	13.	i	6.	a
9.	b	14.	g	7.	n
10.	m	15.	c	8.	b
11.	c	16.	t	9.	m
12.	e	17.	p	10.	l
13.	h	18.	s	11.	i
14.	i	19.	q	12.	f
15.	k	20.	r	13.	d
				14.	g
	Proverbs			15.	e
1.	g				
2.	d				
3.	j				
4.	b				
5.	a				
6.	i				
7.	c				
8.	e				
9.	f				
10.	h				

Answers to Random Review

Daniel / Hosea / Joel / Amos / Obadiah / Jonah

1. e
2. h
3. a
4. c
5. g
6. d
7. b
8. f

Micah / Nahum / Habbakuk / Zechariah / Malachi

1. h
2. d
3. f
4. a
5. j
6. b
7. i
8. g
9. c
10. e

Matthew

1. h
2. d
3. f
4. j
5. a
6. i
7. c
8. b
9. g
10. e

Mark / John / Luke

1. h
2. e
3. g
4. a
5. c
6. i
7. d
8. f

Acts / Romans

1. h
2. j
3. m
4. d
5. a
6. f
7. b
8. k
9. c
10. i
11. e
12. g
13. l

Corinthians

1. c
2. e
3. d
4. a
5. b

Galatians / Ephesians / Phillipians / Collosians

1. f
2. a
3. d
4. b
5. c
6. e

Timothy I & II / Titus James / Peter II

1. d
2. a
3. c
4. b
5. e

325

Answers to "Try These"

Answers to "Try These"

BOOK	CHAPTER	VERSE	WORD
GENESIS	3	15	ENMITY
	9	11	COVENANT
	15	16	INIQUITY
EXODUS	7	18	LOATHE
	15	8	CONGEALED
	29	33	ATONEMENT
LEVITICUS	6	2	EXTORTED
	11	4	CLOVEN
	24	11	BLASPHEMED
NUMBERS	14	18	TRANSGRESSION
	22	30	DISPOSED
DEUTERONOMY	2	30	OBSTINATE
	23	1	EMASCULATED
JOSHUA	8	10	MUSTERED
JUDGES	6	4	SUSTENANCE
	16	21	FETTERS
SAMUEL I	3	13	VILE
SAMUEL II	20	12	WALLOWED
KINGS I	18	21	FALTER
KINGS II	15	20	EXACTED
CHRONICLES I	11	23	WRESTED
CHRONICLES II	6	23	RETRIBUTION
	16	12	MALADY
EZRA	4	15	INCITED
NEHEMIAH	4	1	INDIGNANT
ESTHER	5	13	AVAILS
JOB	8	13	HYPOCRITE
	19	13	ESTRANGED
PSALMS	17	2	VINDICATION
	66	17	EXTOLLED
PROVERBS	1	6	ENIGMA
	6	25	ALLURE

Answers to "Try These"

BOOK	CHAPTER	VERSE	WORD
ECCLESIASTES	10	1	PUTREFY
SONG OF SOLOMON	8	6	VEHEMENT
ISAIAH	10	27	YOKE
	14	27	ANNUL
JEREMIAH	31	14	SATIATE
LAMENTATIONS	2	14	DELUSIONS
EZEKIEL	14	9	INDUCED
EZEKIEL	27	19	TRAVERSING
DANIEL	3	27	SINGED
JOEL	7	6	WRITHE
OBADIAH	1	15	REPRISAL
MICAH	3	7	ABASHED
ZECHARIAH	14	2	RIFLED
MATTHEW	3	12	WINNOWING
	7	15	RAVENOUS
	26	28	REMISSION
LUKE	15	13	PRODIGAL
	21	34	CAROUSING
JOHN	17	12	PERDITION
ACTS	21	20	MYRIADS
ROMANS	11	8	STUPOR
CORINTHIANS I	12	25	SCHISM
CORINTHIANS II	2	17	PEDDLING
	9	1	SUPERFLOUS
GALATIANS	2	4	STEALTH
EPHESIANS	4	31	CLAMOR
TIMOTHY I	6	5	DESTITUTE
TITUS	2	10	PILFERING
JAMES	3	9	SIMILITUDE

Request for Speaking Engagements & Motivational Workshops

To: Comptex Associates, Incorporated
P.O. Box 6745
Washington, D.C.

I have read the entire guide. I am experiencing problems with the following.

_____

_____

I think the information in the guide needs to be altered regarding.

_____

_____

Please contact my high school, church, or organization. You are needed as a motivational speaker and / or workshop leader.

Name:_____

School:_____

Organization:_____

Address:_____

Phone:_____